Indigenous
Confluences

Charlotte Coté and Coll Thrush, *Series Editors*

A DRUM IN ONE HAND, A SOCKEYE IN THE OTHER

Stories of Indigenous Food Sovereignty
from the Northwest Coast

CHARLOTTE COTÉ

UNIVERSITY OF WASHINGTON PRESS

Seattle

A Drum in One Hand, a Sockeye in the Other was made possible in part by generous gift from Jill and Joseph McKinstry and from the Hugh and Jane Ferguson Foundation.

www.tulalipcares.org

This book was supported by the Tulalip Tribes Charitable Fund, which provides the opportunity for a sustainable and healthy community for all.

UNIVERSITY OF WASHINGTON PRESS
uwapress.uw.edu

LIBRARY OF CONGRESS CATALOGING-IN-PUBLICATION DATA
Names: Coté, Charlotte, author.
Title: A drum in one hand, a sockeye in the other : stories of indigenous food sovereignty from the Northwest Coast / Charlotte Coté.
Other titles: Indigenous confluences.
Description: Seattle : University of Washington Press, [2021] | Series: Indigenous confluences | Includes bibliographical references and index.
Identifiers: LCCN 2021013929 (print) | LCCN 2021013930 (ebook) |
ISBN 9780295749518 (hardcover) | ISBN 9780295749525 (paperback) |
ISBN 9780295749532 (ebook)
Subjects: LCSH: Nootka Indians—Food—Tseshaht First Nation. |
Food sovereignty—British Columbia—Port Alberni. | Indigenous peoples—Food—British Columbia—Port Alberni.
Classification: LCC E99.N85 C67 2021 (print) | LCC E99.N85 (ebook) |
DDC 971.1004/97955—dc23
LC record available at https://lccn.loc.gov/2021013929
LC ebook record available at https://lccn.loc.gov/2021013930

This book is dedicated to the warriors for Indigenous food sovereignty, cultural and language revitalization, and environmental and social justice, who have the audacity to dream of a better and healthier future and a world filled with joy.

X̲eekoo, thank you!

CONTENTS

PREFACE

haʔum, We Are What We Eat

ʔukłaamaḥ łuutiismaʔuƛ, ʔuḥuksiƛa mamałḥiqiic ʕimtii Charlotte. ċišaaʔaq-supsi ʔaḥʔaaʔaƛ nuučaaṅułʔaqsup. histaqšiƛsi ċuumaʕas. My name is łuutiis-maʔuƛ, which means "carrying thunder." My English name is Charlotte. I am Tseshaht and Nuu-chah-nulth. I come from an area known as Somass in the English language, which is recognized as the city of Port Alberni.

I am from the whaling lineage of sayaačapis, who was my great-great grandfather and wiitsaḥẁiłim, my great-great grandmother. My maternal great grandparents were ʔapṗikuʔis Watty Watts and ƛuuyaaẏaqšiił Eva Thomas. My grandparents were hiiščatimiik Hughie Watts and Grace Watts. My parents were maḥima Evelyn Georg and Jack Georg.[1] I was born and raised in my village of Tseshaht, which is one of the fourteen autonomous communities that make up the Nuu-chah-nulth Nation, people who are connected through language, culture, and a tradition of hunting whales. Our traditional territory is along the west coast of Vancouver Island in British Columbia.

On many weekends during the summer months when I was a young girl, my grandpa Hughie would drive to the fishing docks in Port Alberni in the late afternoon when the fishermen would be coming in with their fresh catch. He would buy a big bucket of whatever seafood was in season—sea urchin, clams, crab, or halibut—and when he got home he would cook these in a big pot on the stove. Once they were cooked he would put everything in the middle of the dinner table and tell all his grandchildren who were there visiting to dig in. I loved this feast my grandpa would prepare for us. Sometimes he would throw a few salmon heads into the mix and then gross us out by eating their eyes. We could never figure out how he could eat something that looked so nasty, and it was not until I was an adult that I attempted to eat a fish eye. And, to my surprise, it tasted wonderful! Today one of my favorite meals is salmon head soup.

I grew up next door to my grandparents and within a very tight-knit extended family. I was raised in a family and community that maintained deep and strong connections to our haʔumštup, variety of traditional foods, such as qaałqaawi, trailing blackberries; saamin, salmon; p̓uuʔi, halibut; muwač, venison; a range of seafood such as t̓uc̓up, sea urchin, and siiḥm̓uu, herring spawn; and many kinds of plants, such as m̓aayi, salmonberry shoots, and qiłcuup, cow parsnip. I learned how to cut, clean, and process salmon when I was a very young girl. My summers were spent picking qaałqaawi with my relatives along the steep ravines in the mountains in our ḥaḥuułi, ancestral homelands, and I have kept up this tradition into adulthood. My family regularly ate haʔum, traditional food, and I was raised with a keen sense of what it meant to be tiič̓aqƛ, holistically healthy. I have continued to make healthy dietary choices throughout my lifetime, and to take a holistic approach to health, making a strong effort to keep physically, emotionally, and spiritually well. I work hard at being healthy, but I am not a fanatic, and there are times when I have had to eat fast food or make an unhealthy food choice, but I am conscious of it when I do this and limit the times I cheat on my diet; or I should say cheat on my health. I am a firm believer in the motto: "You are what you eat." So throughout my lifetime I have made a great effort to stay connected to our haʔum by harvesting and processing salmon, one of our main staple foods, harvesting plants and medicines, and eating organic and nutritious foods.

I feel fortunate to have been raised to be health conscious because, throughout my lifetime, I have seen a dramatic decrease in the health of my community and in the health of many of my relatives. Where we once fed our children plates filled with nutritious traditional meals of salmon and other seafood, and berries and other plants that grew in our ḥaḥuułi, I began to see community members and relatives become more and more addicted to processed foods, to fast food and to soft drinks, foods that are nutritionally unhealthy. What brought us down this unhealthy road? This question sparked the research and writing of this book. This question becomes even more important as our global society faces a major health crisis with a worldwide pandemic.

In this book I share many of our Nuu-chah-nulth words, especially our words for the variety of ha?um that we harvest in our territory. I was introduced to these names when I was a young girl, and for many years I did not know the English names for our ha?um such as ṫućup, siiḥṁuu, ṁaayi, and qiⱡcuup, and I have continued to refer to them by their Nuu-chah-nulth names. Today many of our community members use the Nuu-chah-nulth names for our ha?um rather than the English equivalent, and their continual use is in itself a significant act of decolonization. Viewed holistically, food, language, culture, and identity are all intertwined; utilizing our Tseshaht words keeps breathing life into our language, reinforces our cultural identity, and is embedded in our Tseshaht philosophy of ḥaćatakma ćawaak—everything is interconnected.[2]

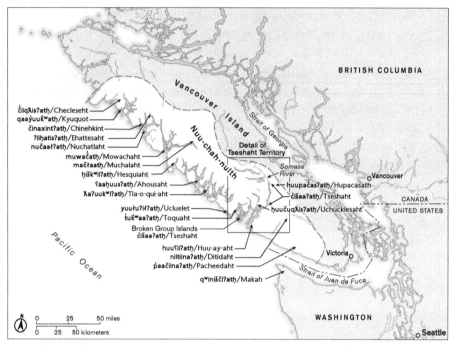

BRITISH COLUMBIA

Vancouver Island

Nuu-chah-nulth

Strait of Georgia

Pacific Ocean

čiiqλis?atḥ/Checleseht
qaaỷuukʷatḥ/Kyuquot
činaxint?atḥ/Chinehkint
ʔiḥatis?atḥ/Ehattesaht
nučaaɫ?atḥ/Nuchatlaht
muwačatḥ/Mowachaht
mačɫaatḥ/Muchalaht
ḥiškʷiiʔatḥ/Hesquiaht
ʕaaḥuus?atḥ/Ahousaht
λa?uukʷiʔatḥ/Tla-o-qui-aht
yuuɫu?iɫ?atḥ/Ucluelet
ɫukʷaa?atḥ/Toquaht
Broken Group Islands
čišaa?atḥ/Tseshaht
huuʕii?atḥ/Huu-ay-aht
niitiina?atḥ/Ditidaht
p̓aačiina?atḥ/Pacheedaht
qʷinišči?atḥ/Makah

Detail of
Tseshaht Territory

Somass
River

huupačas?atḥ/Hupacasath
čišaa?atḥ/Tseshaht
huučuqλis?atḥ/Uchucklesaht

Vancouver

CANADA
UNITED STATES

Victoria

Strait of Juan de Fuca

WASHINGTON

Seattle

N
0   25   50 miles
0   25   50 kilometers

Map of Nuu-chah-nulth territory. *Created by Ben Pease with assistance from Darrell Ross Sr.*

Map of Tseshaht territory. *Created by Ben Pease with assistance from Darrell Ross Sr.*

ACKNOWLEDGMENTS

ƛeekoo

Many people have encouraged, supported, and guided me during the process of researching and writing and have helped me shape my ideas, theories, methodology, and stories into this book. ʔuušýakšiƛeʔicuu. ʕatiqšiƛmiḥsamaḥ siiwa, you have all done something good and I want to acknowledge all of you.

First, I want to thank my wonderful family. When I had doubt, you were always there to lift me up, to provide love and encouragement and to keep me grounded in my culture. nučḥakaḥ čišaaʔaqsup, siiwaaqḥsuu ḥaaḥuupa, quʔiiýap siýa. I am a proud Tseshaht woman because of your teachings. ƛeekoo Uncle Rudy and Aunty Marilyn for your love and support and for always being willing to help me and Gail with fishing, teaching me how to smoke salmon, and providing your smokehouse whenever I need it. A heartfelt thank you to Aunty Millie for your love and always checking in on me to make sure I am doing okay. And a warm thanks to Aunty Matilda for your love and help with finding Nuu-chah-nulth nutritional information.

To my sister Gail, your love, strength, and commitment to keeping our Tseshaht community strong and healthy empowers and inspires me. To my cousin Lisa, you are my rock. When I am feeling stressed you are always there to tell me, "It's going to be okay. You got this." Sis Charlene, ƛeekoo for your love and encouragement. To my cousin Lena and husband Darrell, I am truly grateful for when we get together and immerse ourselves in our culture and language. Darrell, I appreciate your help in finding information on our haʔum, traditional foods, and for assisting me with the map designs. X̌eekoo to my nephews Darrell Jr. and Ed, and my cousin Melanie for providing your awesome photos. Ed, I am so happy we used your beautiful photo of sis Gail at our family beach for the book cover.

Many relatives I write about in this book have passed on but have left me with wonderful memories and the cultural and foods knowledge they instilled in me throughout my lifetime. To my beautiful mom Evelyn, my wonderful grandparents Grace and Hughie, and my amazing aunty Misbun—sharing these stories helps keep all of you in my heart. To all my relatives, I could not have written this book without your love and support, and I am truly blessed to have all of you in my life.

To the Tseshaht, Nuu-chah-nulth, and Northwest Coast people who shared your cultural and foods knowledge with me while sitting together at Potlatches, at Tribal Canoe Journeys, or just sharing a meal or talking around the table, and especially to Sharon, Linda, Les, Richard, Laura, Shaunee, Patricia, Cathy and Kalilah, I am truly grateful to you for sharing your stories with me. In particular, I want to extend my deepest thanks to Nitanis, John, and your incredible family. You inspire me with your warrior spirit and your commitment to living a life grounded in our foodways, language, and cultural traditions. And a special thanks for sharing your photos.

For assistance with Nuu-chah-nulth words and phrases, I extend a heartfelt X̌eekoo to Adam Werle, Della Preston, and my cousins Linsey and Lena. I also want to thank Denise Titian, Debbie Preston, and my late Uncle Bob for your photos.

I extend my deepest appreciation to the University of Washington Press for your collective support and direction. A special thank you to UW Press editorial director Larin McLaughlin for your support and patience, and to my Indigenous Confluence Series coeditor Coll Thrush for your insight and guidance. In addition, I want to thank the anonymous reviewers for your helpful comments and thorough reviews of my manuscript. I also want to thank former UW Press senior acquisitions editor Ranjit Arab, who gave me encouragement as I pursued this book project and continued to provide me with editorial support in seeing my manuscript to fruition.

I express my sincere gratitude to the University of Washington's Department of American Indian Studies (AIS), the Center for American Indian/Indigenous Studies, and the Canadian Studies Program for funding and grant support. A special thanks to my AIS colleagues and staff for your support and encouragement. To all my students, your enthusiasm for learning about Indigenous food sovereignty motivates me to keep doing this work.

To my Seattle sister Cynthia del Rosario, Dian Million, Dana Arviso, Jessica Salvador, Susan Balbas, Jean Dennison, Stephanie Fryberg, Augustine McCaffery, Cheryl Metoyer, Michelle Montgomery, Clarita Lefthand Begay, and Katie Bunn-Marcuse, I raise my hands to all of you in thanks and appreciation for your guidance and reassurance and, most of all, for your love and friendship.

Lastly, x̣eekoo to all my food sovereignty and environmental justice friends and warriors, Nitanis Desjarlais, Dawn Morrison, Mariaelena Huambachano, Elizabeth Hoover, Valerie Segrest, Joyce LeCompte, Michelle Daigle, Fiona Wiremu, and Mate Heitia, your passion and dedication to creating healthy Indigenous nations will continue to fuel and nurture my research and writing.

x̣eekoo, thank you all for sharing in my journey. ʔuušy̓akšiƛeʔicuu.

PHONETIC KEY

The Nuu-chah-nulth alphabet that is more or less standard today on the west coast of Vancouver Island was established in the work *Our World, Our Ways: Taataaqsapa Cultural Dictionary*, published by the Nuu-chah-nulth Tribal Council in 1991. It is an Americanist phonetic alphabet, slightly adapted from the alphabet used in anthropologist-linguist Edward Sapir and linguist Morris Swadesh's book *Nootka Texts*. University of Victoria linguist and language activist ƛiisƛi-isaʔapt Dr. Adam Werle says the Taataaqsapa dictionary mistakenly declares that the Nuu-chah-nulth alphabet is "a modified form of the International Phonetic Alphabet" (IPA). He notes that there is no direct connection between the Nuu-chah-nulth alphabet and the IPA.

The Nuu-chah-nulth spellings and definitions of our words that I use in this book were provided by Dr. Werle with assistance from Tseshaht members yaacuuʔisʔaqs Linsey Haggard and čiisma Della Preston. I use these words in their Nuu-chah-nulth spellings as a way to empower our language and resist colonialism, rather than respelling them in English. Language, culture, and identity are intertwined, and as our Indigenous languages become more endangered, it becomes more critical that we keep our languages alive. As described in the epilogue, in June 2020 I began taking online language classes with Dr. Werle and other Nuu-chah-nulth language learners, and my language journey continues to the present.

Following is a sound chart to help non-Nuu-chah-nulth readers. For a list of all of the Nuu-chah-nulth words used, see the glossary at the back of the book.

a	sounds like the "a" in *what*
aa	sounds like a long, drawn-out "a," as in *father*
c	sounds like the "ts" in *hats*
ċ	a glottalized sound, like "ts" but pronounced forcefully
č	sounds like the "ch" in *church*
č̓	a glottalized sound, like "ch" but pronounced forcefully
e	has the sound in *pet*
ee	has the sound in *eggs*
h	has the sound in *house*
ḥ	sounds like an "h" made deep in the throat like when breathing on glasses to clean them
i	sounds like the "i" in *it*
ii	sounds like a long "e," as in *greed*
k	sounds like the "k" in *kite*
kʷ	sounds like the "qu" in *quick*
k̓	a glottalized sound, like "k" but pronounced forcefully
k̓ʷ	a glottalized sound, like "qu" but pronounced forcefully
ł	the barred "l," a hissed version of "l," resembling the English "th" sound
ƛ	the barred lambda, sounds like "tl"
ƛ̓	a glottalized sound, like "tl" but pronounced forcefully
m	sounds like the "m" in *mother*
m̓	a glottalized sound, like "m" but pronounced forcefully
n	sounds like the "n" in *nose*

ṅ	a glottalized sound, like "n" but pronounced forcefully
oo	has the sound as in *paw*
p	sounds like "p" in *pig*
ṗ	a glottalized sound, like "p" but pronounced forcefully
q	sounds like a "k" made deep in the throat
qʷ	sounds like a "k" made deep in the throat with a "w"
s	has the sound in *six*
š	sounds like the "sh" in *shoe*
t	sounds like the "t" in *toast*
ṫ	a glottalized sound, like "t" but pronounced forcefully
u	has the sound in *took*
uu	has the sound in *boot*
w	sounds like the "w" in *wood*
ẇ	a glottalized sound, like "w" but pronounced forcefully
x	the front "x," sounds like a cat's hiss
xʷ	like the front "x" but with a "w"
x̣	the back "x," a sound from the back of your throat, like clearing phlegm
x̣ʷ	like the back "x" but with a "w"
y	sounds like the "y" in *yes*
ẏ	a glottalized sound, like "y" but pronounced forcefully
ʔ	the glottal stop, a closing of the vocal chords
ʕ	the pharyngeal stop, made by tensing the throat as if being strangled

A DRUM IN ONE HAND,
A SOCKEYE IN THE OTHER

ḥačatakma ċawaak

Everything Is Interconnected

I BEGIN this book with a story of one of my favorite pastimes, picking qaał-qaawi, wild blackberries, with my relatives. This story comes from a 2012 berry-picking adventure with my Aunty Misbun.

Shut Up! We're Bonding!

On a hot summer day, my Aunty Misbun and I were out doing what we had always done since I was a young girl—we were driving on winding, dusty gravel roads up steep mountains in the ḥaḥuułi, ancestral homelands, of my people the Tseshaht, on the west coast of Vancouver Island, on our quest for the sweet and delectable qaałqaawi, wild trailing blackberry. These qaałqaawi are quite different than the tupkaapiiḥ, Himalayan blackberry, that were brought here from Europe and grow alongside the roads close to urban centers. The qaałqaawi is much smaller, hardier, and considerably richer in antioxidants than its tame cousins and is high in vitamin C, potassium, magnesium, and other flavonoid phytochemicals. It grows high in the mountains in flat areas within the dense coastal rainforests that blanket the Northwest Coast.[1]

It almost seems like a misnomer to call qaałqaawi "wild." The Nuu-chah-nulth-aht (Nuu-chah-nulth people), like other Indigenous peoples, cultivated lands in our ḥaḥuułi to encourage growth of certain food plants, and this was done through sophisticated selective and controlled burning, promoting the growth and production of berry vines.[2] But through colonization and forced placement on reserve lands we lost many of our traditional harvesting sites, which fell under the control of forestry companies, and as a result, we lost our ability to engineer the lands for production. However, this ancestral knowledge continued to be transferred through the generations, and my grandfather Hughie Watts (Aunty Misbun's father) was raised with the understanding and ecological knowledge of land burning. Grandpa would drive through our former harvesting sites and take note of where the forestry companies were slash burning to remove the underbrush, to make it easier to cut trees and remove the fallen logs. He knew that in a few years these would be ideal growing areas for the qaałqaawi.

Grandpa passed on his cultural knowledge to us, especially the knowledge of where to find the best ńačyuu or berry patch. But this afternoon was not the day for finding a good ńačyuu, and there we were, hours later, still looking for one. The day shifted into the late afternoon and I was getting tired of looking for qaałqaawi, what seemed to be a hopeless situation. I was about ready to tell my aunty we should just give up and go home. And then my aunty steered around a slight bend in the gravel road and there it was, a few yards ahead of us on the right side of the road—a ńačyuu! My aunt slammed on the vehicle brakes and hastily pulled over to the side of the narrow road. Since the sun was already going down on this side of the mountain, we needed to hurry. We grabbed our berry-picking pails out of the trunk of the car and ran to the small patch of ripe, deep purple qaałqaawi just waiting to be plucked from their hardy vines. I found a comfortable spot close to the road and Aunty Misbun made her way through the vines to start picking from the other side of the patch, about twenty feet away. And then we began plucking berries to our hearts' content. My head was down, my fingers were going a mile a minute, and my thoughts were lost in berry-picking heaven.

We had been picking for about fifteen minutes when I suddenly felt my aunt rush past me. I pulled my head up from the vines to ask what the heck was going on. "What's the matter?" I queried. Sometimes when we were picking berries we would run into bears that were also enjoying a berry feast, and while they usually did not bother us, we had to be cautious if we encountered a mother with her cubs, as she likely did not want us to come close to them. But I looked around and did not see any.

"Bees, bees!" Aunty Misbun yelled, madly swatting at the air around her head as she ran toward our vehicle. My aunt had stepped right into the middle of a nest. "What the hell!" I gasped. I grabbed my pail and stumbled to my feet, spilling all the juicy berries I was dreaming about eating when I got home. I sprinted behind my aunt while swatting at the bees that were now after me. We got to the vehicle and jumped inside. Aunty Misbun started the car and we drove off leaving behind the bees—and leaving behind most of our qaałqaawi. By this time, I had had enough and was ready to call it a day. I was tired, I was hungry, and I was aching from the couple of bee stings I received. But not my Aunty Misbun. She wanted her qaałqaawi, and the broiling sun, dust, dirt, hunger, and a few bee stings were not going to keep her from getting them.

I looked at my aunt and said, "It's hopeless. Why don't we just go home? This is crazy. We're never going to find any more berries!" My aunt responded, "Shut up! We're bonding!" And, with a trickle of sweat running down her cheek, a slight smile on her lips, and a persistent look in her eyes, she continued driving up the mountain . . .

Talking around the Table: Story as Theory and Methodology

In this book I share this story of picking qaałqaawi with my Aunty Misbun and many other stories about our Tseshaht and Northwest Coast Indigenous food traditions, because I want readers to understand why we, Tseshaht, and Indigenous peoples worldwide, are revitalizing our foodways and reconnecting with our haʔum, traditional food, by enacting food sovereignty. Enacting food sovereignty is positioned within our struggles for decolonization and self-determination and is central to restoring health and wellness in our Indigenous communities. This book is framed in narratives, discourse, conversations, and stories that have been shared with me over many years. These stories center on our traditional foods, and although the term "traditional" can be a loaded term in some contexts, I use it as a way to discuss foods we have used for long periods of time, foods that are connected to our Indigenous identities. Some scholars choose to use the term "first foods," but many of the foods we eat were not our original foods. For example, my people ate mostly foods from the sea and supplanted our marine-based diet with animals such as deer and elk. Today we recognize deer and elk as traditional foods. So what is Indigenous food? There is no one box into which all Indigenous foods fit. Every Indigenous culture has its own traditional foods and food traditions, practices, and ceremonies unique to its own cultural identity and geographic location and that played a role in the development of these foodways.

In framing my book within Indigenous narratives, I cultivate a foods history that centers our voices and positions our bodies as libraries of cultural knowledge passed down from generations of ancestors and kept alive through the telling, sharing, experiencing, and remembering. Indigenous storytelling is an act of resistance and is a form of decolonization. Centering Indigenous narrative challenges settler colonialism, which, as Yellowknives Dene scholar Glen Coulthard explains, "refers to the dispossession of Indigenous peoples from their lands."[3] This dispossession, as scholars Eve Tuck (Aleut/Unangax) and K. Wayne Yang articulate, "operates through internal/external colonial modes simultaneously because there is no special separation between metropole and colony.[4] Settler colonialism, as contrasted with colonialism, includes both "displacement and replacement."[5] And as Tuck and Yang explain, "settlers come with the intention of making a new home on the land, a homemaking that insists on settler society over all things in their new domain. . . . In order for settlers to make their home, they must destroy and disappear Indigenous peoples that live there. . . . Indigenous peoples must be erased, must be made into ghosts." This erasure includes stripping Indigenous peoples of our self-determining authority, as Coulthard asserts.[6]

The colonial erasure goes beyond removing Indigenous peoples from our lands, waters, and foods; it was just as much about silencing our voices, erasing our ability to pass on our cultural knowledge, and then having the ethnocentric belief that settler society could, and should, speak for us. "It galls us," writes Maori scholar Linda Tuhiwai Smith, "that Western researchers and intellectuals can assume to know all that it is possible to know of us" and "can desire, extract and claim ownership of our ways of knowing . . . and then simultaneously reject the people who created and developed those ideas." Smith continues, "It angers us when practices . . . are still employed to deny the validity of indigenous peoples' claims to existence, to land and territories, to the right of self-determination, to the survival of our languages and forms of cultural knowledge, to our natural resources and systems for living within our environments."[7] This is why we Indigenous peoples need to speak out, speak back, and resist having our voices silenced while at the same time creating spaces where our voices can be centered, heard, and respected.

In many ways, it is not surprising that a book centered in Indigenous knowledge, experience, and history is told through a methodology of storytelling. Indigenous peoples come from oral traditions, where our knowledge, theories, and epistemological frameworks were developed, maintained, and transferred from one generation to the next. Stories are both individual and communal. They are grounded in our own personal lived experiences, while simultaneously connecting us to our families, communities, and cultures in a deep and profound way. As Cree/Saulteaux scholar Margaret Kovach explains, "Stories remind us of who we are and of our belonging. Stories hold within them knowledges while simultaneously signifying relationships. . . . [Stories] tie us to our past and provide a basis for continuity with future generations."[8]

Situating storytelling within the context of decolonizing academic and legal institutions, Aborigine scholar Larissa Behrendt says, "[I]t is a way of asserting Indigenous voice, perspective, and experience. Storytelling is an act of sovereignty that reinforces Indigenous identity, values, and worldviews."[9] Storytelling is "a transformative practice," writes Behrendt, and plays a key role in the assertion of our sovereignty and in countering colonial narratives. Storytelling as methodology and as a source of knowledge counters structural privileges embedded in academic institutions which, as Behrendt maintains, "have been unwelcoming and alienating for Indigenous people and in disciplines that have privileged colonial perspectives over Indigenous ones."[10] Indigenous storytelling challenges the Western colonial academic paradigm, and telling stories is a powerful act of resistance.

So we speak back and write about what we want to talk about, and what we want to share with the outside world. The stories we tell and the stories we hear help shape who we are.

My methodology is centered in community-based, participatory research or, as I like to call it, "talking around the table." Many of the stories I share in this book come from stories I heard at our Potlatch feasts, stories I heard at our communal Fish Day (which I write about in chapter 2), stories I heard sitting at the table while sharing a meal with relatives or community members, and stories from my own lived experience. I share these stories as theory of who we are as Tseshaht, as Nuu-chah-nulth-aht, as Indigenous people. Our stories, as Athabascan scholar Dian Million writes, are powerful:

I am exceedingly aware that our stories, whether they are told from painful secrets in an AA meeting, as traditional oral performance, or those we tell each other in these academic settings, are powerful. They are powerful because they are engaged in the articulations that interpret who we are in the discursive relations of our times. We engage in questioning and reformulating those stories that account for the relations of power in our present. That is theorizing. It offers new experiential frames, in our case, often from our lives, from our own felt experience, from our stories, from our communities, from our languages. Most important, from our experiences, from our lives, from our "what happened." Theory is always practical first, rather than abstract.[11]

Tseshaht ontology, our way of being, is expressed through ḥačatakma ćawaak (also written as hišukʔiš ćawaak),[12] that everything in our world is interconnected and informs how we understand the world through our voices, through our pain, through our strength, and through our wisdom. Our stories are places of contention, of cultural learning, of spiritual and emotional seeking, and of strength. Indigenous stories and storytelling within Indigenous epistemologies are, as Sium and Ritskes explain, sustaining and knowledge producing, but they can also be disruptive, an act "of living resistance."[13] Indigenous stories are what Million so aptly explicates as Indigenous theory "in action."[14]

Reframing Food Sovereignty within the Context of Tseshaht/Nuu-chah-nulth Philosophy and Ontology

Throughout this book I endeavor to frame Tseshaht ecological and foods knowledge discourse around Tseshaht/Nuu-chah-nulth philosophies of ʔiisaak, being respectful; ʔuʔaałuk, to take care of; and ḥačatakma ćawaak, everything is interconnected, principles that guide our relationships to our natural and spiritual worlds. Embodied in these philosophies is the understanding that we must honor the wisdom and values of ancestral knowledge in maintaining responsible and respectful relationships with the environment. Our principle of ʔiisaak applies to all life forms as well as to the land and water and, at its most basic understanding, teaches that all life forms are held in equal esteem. Our relationships to the plants and animals that give themselves as food derives from ʔiisaak, which enforces sustainability and places sanctions on those who are stingy or wasteful.[15] The underlying vision of ʔuʔaałuk is to "take care of" the ḥaḥuułi, ancestral homelands, in a way that is consistent with Nuu-chah-nulth values and principles, a responsibility given to our people through n̓aas,[16] our Creator. The principles of ʔiisaak and ʔuʔaałuk are embedded within an overarching philosophy of ḥaċatakma ċawaak (hišukʔiš ċawaak), meaning "everything is interconnected."

In his book *Tsawalk: A Nuu-chah-nulth Worldview*, Nuu-chah-nulth hereditary chief Umeek, Richard Atleo, defines an ontology drawn from Nuu-chah-nulth origin stories to explain how our philosophy of ḥaċatakma ċawaak (hišukʔiš ċawaak) is embedded in a Nuu-chah-nulth worldview. In viewing the universe as a "network of relationships," ḥaċatakma ċawaak represents the unity of the physical and metaphysical in a relationship embodied in the principle of ʔiisaak.[17] This philosophy connects people, animals, plants, and the natural and the supernatural or spiritual realms in a seamless and interconnected web of life where all life forms are revered and worthy of mutual respect. The land, water, animals, and plants are regarded as your kinfolk, not as a commodity that can be exploited.[18]

The stewardship of our homelands was rooted in this philosophy that Umeek articulates in his book, and this is what we are striving to revitalize. Nuu-chah-nulth hereditary chief Tom Mexsis Happynook maintains that embedded within these human and nonhuman relations is the understanding of responsibilities that Indigenous peoples strive to uphold in our social, cultural, and economic practices, responsibilities that over millennia have evolved into unwritten laws: "These responsibilities and laws are directly tied to nature" and a product of "the slow integration of cultures within their environment and the ecosystems." Thus, Happynook says, "the environment is not a place of divisions but rather a place of relations, a place where cultural diversity and bio-diversity are not separate but in fact need each other."[19] This is cultural biodiversity that has developed and been nurtured over millennia and is the basis of Nuu-chah-nulth philosophy ḥaċatakma ċawaak (hišukʔiš ċawaak) that everything in our natural and spiritual worlds is interconnected.[20]

Positioning This Book within the Indigenous Foods and Foods Sovereignty Movements

For thousands of years before contact with Europeans, Indigenous people held autonomy over their food systems and maintained food security through a rich knowledge of their environment and food resources, passed down through oral tradition and long-standing land stewardship and cultivation practices.[21] Reviving and restoring our Indigenous foodways is directly linked to decolonization by resisting Western and unhealthy foods that were forced on us—forms of culinary imperialism and food hegemony. Re-Indigenizing our diets is at the heart of the cultural resurgence and revitalization movements we are witnessing in our communities today. In the early 1990s we saw the birth of the food sovereignty movement, and scholars throughout the world began framing their theory and ideas around global food security and insecurity.

The growing Indigenous foods and food sovereignty movements are positioned within the larger anti-colonial struggle to decolonize our homelands, our bodies, our diets, and our taste buds and rebuild and strengthen cultural and sacred relationships to the plants, animals, and ecosystems that provide us with healthy and nutritious foods. In this book, I attempt to center the work of many Indigenous scholars who are cultivating academic spaces for our voices to be heard and connecting these to the important work being done in our communities. Focusing on Indigenous food sovereignty in the United States, Devon Mihesuah and Elizabeth Hoover's edited volume *Indigenous Food Sovereignty in the United States: Restoring Cultural Knowledge and Protecting Environments and Regaining Health* (2019) draws together Indigenous voices from throughout the United States who articulate their understanding of food sovereignty and its potential for strengthening Indigenous food traditions and restoring health and wellness in Indigenous communities.[22] Similarly, in Canada, Shailesh Shukla and Priscilla Settee's edited volume *Indigenous Food Systems: Concepts, Cases, and Conversations* (2020) explores Indigenous food systems across Canada and includes Indigenous and non-Indigenous voices whose academic and community-based work seeks to reinforce the importance of revitalizing Indigenous foodways for both the health and well-being of Indigenous and Canadian populations.[23]

While not focusing exclusively on Indigenous food traditions or food sovereignty, Robin Kimmerer's *Braiding Sweetgrass: Indigenous Wisdom, Scientific Knowledge, and the Teachings of Plants* (2013) is a significant contribution to this canon in how it weaves together Indigenous ecological knowledge and science to create an understanding of the reciprocal relationships that Indigenous peoples have to their plant and animal relatives, and to view the sustenance they provide as gifts that must be honored and returned.[24] Meanwhile, Enrique Salmón's book *Eating the Landscape: American Indian Stories of Food, Identity, and*

Resilience (2012) brings readers on a journey through the southwestern United States and northern Mexico to illuminate how Indigenous agricultural foodways are embedded in traditional ecological knowledge practices and deeply connected to culture and identity.[25] An important book to come out of the Pacific Northwest is Elise Krohn and Valerie Segrest's *Feeding the People, Feeding the Spirit: Revitalizing Northwest Coastal Indian Food Culture* (2010), which was written specifically for Indigenous people working in their communities around health and traditional foods revitalization and examines pre-contact coastal Indigenous food traditions, the impact of colonization on traditional foodways, and the revival of coastal food traditions as told through the voices, stories, photos, and recipes from the Indigenous peoples in the Pacific Northwest.[26] In the following chapter I provide further analysis of some of these publications as well as the food sovereignty work of other Indigenous scholars such as Dawn Morrison, Mariaelena Huambachano, and Michelle Daigle, whose community-based research has greatly contributed to the food studies canon and food sovereignty scholarship. My book seeks to expand on this important scholarship and provide a valuable contribution that is centered in the Northwest Coast.

Food Security, Health, and COVID-19

Doing the research for this book made me think a lot about healing and how historical trauma is deeply embedded in our collective Indigenous experience. I explore healing in many ways; our individual and collective physical, emotional, and spiritual healing, or what we Tseshaht define as tiičʕaqƛ, holistic health. I also think through this in relation to healing the nisma, land, and our relationship to it. As Indigenous peoples, we live in a world of reciprocal relationships with the plants and animals that provide us with food, clothing, shelter, and cultural and spiritual sustenance. In return, we treat plants, animals, water, land, and air as "gifts" from the Creator, and we are bound by a "covenant of reciprocity," as scientist and plant ecologist Robin Kimmerer (Citizen Potawatomi Nation) so aptly asserts in her inspiring book, *Braiding Sweetgrass*. Colonialism forced us into capitalist-driven societies that cultivated a culture based on greed, which devastated these harmonious, sustainable, and healthy relationships that kept our cultures in balance. Decolonization, therefore, necessitates healing; healing ourselves, and healing and rebuilding healthy relationships with the nisma and everything it provides to us as gifts—we must be good medicine for each other.

As I finish the final edits for this manuscript we are still in the midst of a historic global pandemic. The worldwide economic and social devastation brought on by the COVID-19 pandemic has revealed the stark contrasts between the fortunate and vulnerable in our societies. While the virus impacts both groups indiscriminately, it is their ability to respond that is unequal. Because of the racial and economic inequities embedded in the United States, as well as in Canada and other countries throughout the world, the effects of the coronavirus are compounded for Indigenous people and people of color. Simply put: many of our Indigenous communities lack the means to reduce the risk of contagion. Major concerns include things like having access to adequate health care, having fresh, clean water to wash our hands, or even having access to hand sanitizer. In our Indigenous communities, people also often live in close quarters with one another, or have many people living under one roof, which makes spreading this type of infectious disease that much easier. All this is made worse by the fact that colonialism continues to undermine our Indigenous societies as we, Indigenous peoples, face continual assaults on our cultural identity and attacks on our indigeneity that negatively impact our emotional and spiritual health.

Many Indigenous Nations across the United States and Canada, including mine, the Nuu-chah-nulth, have been hit hard by the coronavirus. In mid-May of 2020 the Navajo Nation in the southwestern United States had the highest per-capita infection rate anywhere in the United States, with 2,304.41 cases of COVID-19 per 100,000 people, out of a population of 173,667.[27] As of January 25, 2021, it has had 26,612 cases with 933 deaths.[28] By the end of 2020 our Nuu-chah-nulth Nation was also facing major spikes in coronavirus cases, leading many of our communities to go into a full lockdown to stop the further spread of the virus. Unofficially, as of January 2021, in the fourteen communities that make up the Nuu-chah-nulth Nation of 10,000 people, we have had approximately 50 people test positive for COVID-19 and 3 people have died.

The media, health officials, and politicians focus on a vaccine and physical distancing to stop the spread of COVID-19. But why has there been little attention to the foods we eat, to nutrition and making ourselves healthy to fight these viruses? As leading medical scholars, doctors, and food advocates point out: "Among the most significant risk factors for hospitalization and death in Covid-19 are the presence of diet-related chronic diseases such as hypertension, heart disease, and obesity. . . . A 2018 study found that only 12% of Americans are metabolically healthy, which is defined as having optimal levels of blood markers and pressures as well as waist circumference. . . . Poor metabolic health stems, in part, from poor-quality diets and poor nutrition."[29] This is the time to question seriously the global industrial foods system with its pesticides and factory farming that also lead to inhumane conditions for the animals locked in pens and cages, pumped with antibiotics that are then passed on to us, through our eating their meat. We need to think even more about the food we eat, now that our global food systems and our health are being threatened.

The Industrial Food System and the Rise of Global Food Insecurity

> Something is broken when the food comes on a Styrofoam tray wrapped in
> slippery plastic, a carcass of a being whose only chance at life
> was a cramped cage. This is not a gift of life; it is a theft.
> —ROBIN KIMMERER, *Braiding Sweetgrass*

The UN's Food and Agricultural Organization (FAO) defines food security as a situation that "exists when all people, at all times, have physical, social and economic access to sufficient, safe, and nutritious food that meets their dietary needs and food preferences for an active and healthy life."[30] But in 2019, of the more than 7.7 billion people in the world, almost half experienced food shortages and food insecurity. This food insecurity largely stems from the global shifts in food production in the mid-eighteenth century, which resulted in a move away from small-scale polyculture farming to a more industrialized and capitalist mode of food production that focused on monoculture agriculture.[31] This movement to a global food system was initiated by industrialized wealthy countries to raise agricultural productivity through infrastructure and research, and government investment and intervention in markets, all of which led to globally standardized agricultural practices and the development of globalized agricapitalism in the early twentieth century.[32] By the end of the century, neoliberal trade policies, supported by the World Bank, the World Trade Organization (WTO), and the International Monetary Fund (IMF), promoted agricultural and food practices aimed at maximizing efficiency, reducing costs, and increasing production.[33] As a result, the world is currently producing more than 1.5 times the food needed to feed every person on the planet, yet a sixth of its population cannot afford the buy this food.[34] In other words, while more food was being produced, agro-ecologist and director of Food First Eric Holt-Giménez says, more people globally were becoming food insecure.[35]

Ironically, the industrialized, globalized food production, with monoculture crop production supported by a chemical-intensive agriculture, was used as justification to "feed the people." However, as environmental activist Vandana Shiva asserts, world hunger was not reduced; in fact, Shiva argues, "the problem of hunger has grown." One billion people worldwide are permanently hungry; another two billion suffer from food-related diseases. When the focus of agriculture is the production of commodities for trade, instead of food for nourishment, hunger and malnutrition are the outcome. Only 10 percent of corn and soy grown in the world are used for human consumption; the rest goes for animal feed and biofuel. As Shiva asserts, commodities do not feed people, food does.[36]

The rise of cheap corn in the 1950s and 1960s made it more profitable for farmers to fatten their animals with corn in feedlots instead of on grass or wheat on an open range, and to raise chickens in large closed-in factories rather than in open farmyards.[37] Corporations paid farmers to mass-produce animals, using steroids to help them grow faster and bigger, and pumped them with antibiotics to keep them from getting sick from the unnatural foods they were being forced to eat.[38] Gone are the farms where cattle and pigs grazed openly on grass, where chickens moved about in large pens eating natural food like earthworms and insects, and hens could take a break from their laying nests and walk freely outside their coops. Corporate factory farming reduced animals to commodities and machines that pump out meat, eggs, and milk in mass quantities.[39]

Settler Colonialism and Indigenous Food Insecurity

The approximately 400 million Indigenous people worldwide face the most serious food insecurity because of the incessant impact of settler colonialism.[40] In examining colonialism and its impact on Indigenous peoples in Canada, Mohawk scholar Taiaiake Alfred says, "Colonialism is best conceptualized as an irresistible outcome of a multigenerational and multifaceted process of forced dispossession and attempted acculturation—a disconnection from land, culture, and community—that has resulted in political chaos and social discord within First Nations communities in Canada and the collective dependency of First Nations upon the state."[41] As Dakota scholar Waziyatawin asserts, "This disconnect was key to the process of colonization," and "Colonial governments worked systematically to break our ancestors' connections to our homelands."[42] The tragic history of colonialism and resulting economic, social, and cultural marginalization has had profound health impacts on Indigenous peoples world-wide. Indigenous women have been the most susceptible to colonialism and its impact on our ancestral lands. Research studies demonstrate a direct correlation of violence against Indigenous homelands with violence directed at Indigenous women. This research has brought attention to gender-based environmental violence and the ongoing harm to Indigenous women's health due to environmental toxins. Iako'tsi:rareh Amanda Lickers (Turtle Clan, Seneca) explains, "If you're destroying and poisoning the things that give us life, the things that shape our identity, the places that we are from and the things that sustain us, then how can you not be poisoning us? How can that not be direct violence against our bodies, whether that be respiratory illness or cancer or liver failure, or the inability to carry children?"[43]

In her research on colonialism and its historical and contemporary impact on Indigenous health, Snohomish scholar Teresa Evans-Campbell explains how colonial practices functioned to colonize, subjugate, and perpetrate ethnocide and genocide against Indigenous peoples.[44] Evans-Campbell characterizes this as cumulative intergenerational trauma, whereby Native Americans suffer from the highest rates of interpersonal violence, child abuse and neglect, poor health, negative stereotypes and microaggressions that denigrate and destabilize their societies and identity, and adversely affect individual and community physical, social, psychological, emotional, and spiritual health and well-being.[45] Much research has been conducted on historical trauma on certain populations, mainly holocaust survivors, but new research focusing on Indigenous peoples, especially research on US and Canadian boarding schools, which I discuss in chapter 3, shows a particular trauma, or wounding, that individuals who attended these schools experienced and that has been passed down to following generations. Scholars argue that colonization, especially in the violent way it was enacted, disrupted protective measures that are engrained in culture, leading to loss of parenting skills, an increase in psychological trauma, and a subsequent rise in health issues.[46]

Loss of homelands, urbanization (more than 50 percent of Indigenous people in Canada and the United States live in urban centers), a decline in traditional harvesting practices, environmental contamination, and more sedentary lifestyles caused major changes to our diets and health, resulting in food insecurity and the rise of disease. Food insecurity for Indigenous peoples goes beyond the current definition that focuses on monetary access to industrial market foods. As health and nutrition scholars Grace Egeland and Gail Harrison note: "Given the role of traditional food systems and food sharing networks in contributing to food security, nutrient intakes and cultural identity, the definition of food security for Indigenous Peoples should include assessment of traditional food intake and the stability of access to traditional foods."[47] Changing environments, climate change, environmental contamination and degradation all impact Indigenous food security along with global market forces and colonization.[48]

The Industrial Food System and Its Impact on Indigenous Health

A 2019 study estimates that one in five deaths globally are associated with the Western diet high in salt, sugar, fat, and high levels of red and processed meats. According to the study, in 2017, 11 million deaths were attributed to a poor diet, creating the highest risk factor, higher than any other factors in the world.[49] Worldwide there has been an increase in disease in the global population. The industrialization and commodification of foods globally has a direct correlation with the rise of disease, which is more specifically linked to the increase in highly processed foods and refined grains, and the use of chemicals to raise crops and animals in monoculture methods.[50] As popular food writer Michael Pollan states, the combination of unnatural diets of corn that animals are fed, and the steroids, antibiotics and other drugs they are given "undermines the health of the human who will eat it. . . . We inhabit the same microbial ecosystem as the animals we eat, and whatever happens to it will also happen to us."[51]

All of our uncertainties about nutrition should not obscure the plain fact that the chronic diseases that now kill us—coronary heart disease, diabetes, stroke, and cancer—can be traced directly to the industrialization of our food: the rise of highly processed foods and refined grains; the use of chemicals to raise plants and animals in huge monocultures; the superabundance of cheap calories of sugar and fat produced by modern agriculture; and the narrowing of the biological diversity of the human diet to a tiny handful of staple crops.[52] Indigenous people bear a disproportionate brunt of this burden of health and social suffering, greater than the general population, because colonization "relates to the disruption of ties to the land and traditional food systems that had an omnipresent role in defining traditional social arrangements, self-identity with defined roles for community members, and systems of knowledge."[53] And as eth-nobiologists Nancy and Katherine Turner write, "Through a complex interplay of colonial pressures and policies, traditional foods were marginalized and their use declined dramatically within the diets of the Northwest Coast First Peoples."[54] While data on industrial food consumption differ among Indigenous peoples and communities, "Indigenous Peoples experience greater rates of health disparities and decreased longevity compared with non-Indigenous Peoples," and as Egeland and Harrison explain, this is "regardless of the geographic area in which they live."[55] The majority of Indigenous diets have been overwhelmed by industrial foods and a Western diet with foods high in salt, sugar, and fat and with traditional foods playing a supplemental role.

A 2013 report on Indigenous health in Canada indicates that Indigenous people experience disproportionate rates of tuberculosis at 26.4 times the rate of the general population. Type 2 diabetes is now considered to have reached "epidemic" levels in Canada's Indigenous communities, where adults are four times as likely to suffer from type 2 diabetes and are more likely to experience health complications related to the disease than are other Canadians.[56] A recent study on Native Americans showed that in 2017, they were almost three times more likely than the non-Hispanic white adult population to be diagnosed with type 2 diabetes.[57] Foods inundated with sugar overwhelm the ability of insulin to process it, leading to type 2 diabetes and all the other chronic diseases associated with metabolic syndromes.[58]

Similarly, the *Strong Heart Study*, which examined Native American health from the 1980s to the present (2019), showed a continual rise in cardiovascular disease, with more than 30 percent of Native American deaths associated with this disease.[59] In looking at Native American health up to 2011, the Indian Health Service shows heart disease and diabetes as the leading causes of death and that Native Americans die from these diseases at a much higher rate than other Americans.[60] Type 2 diabetes leads to other illnesses and health concerns, such as cardiovascular disease, kidney failure, blindness, lower-extremity amputation, disability, and a decreased quality of life. The risk of developing type 2 diabetes increases with obesity and physical inactivity, which is a concern not only for adults but for children as well, with recent studies revealing serious youth obesity problems in Indigenous communities, leading to major health issues such as type 2 diabetes and heart disease as they age.[61]

Colonizing Our Diets and Tastebuds

Prior to colonization, traditional hunting, fishing and gathering activities provided nutrient-rich diets to Indigenous communities. Dependent on what was available in the geographic area, these diets were high in animal proteins, animal fats, and fat-soluble vitamins. They also contained lots of plant sources such as wild rice, tubers, chenopods, beans, seeds, maize, squash, berries, and leafy vegetables.[62] Post-colonization, however, there has been a continual shift in Indigenous diets toward processed foods.[63] Like everyone else, Indigenous people were also pulled into the savvy marketing of multi-billion-dollar capitalist corporations to get their industrialized, processed foods on our tables and into our diets. In the United States food companies spent millions of dollars calculating their foods' "bliss points," finding the exact amounts of salt, sugar, and fat needed to enhance our craving for these foods.[64] The widespread acceleration of this Western diet was designed to give instant gratification: when processed foods are ingested, the blood gets besieged with high levels of salt, sugar, and fat, causing the brain to react the same way it reacts to narcotics, following the same neurological circuitry to reach the brain's pleasure zones, the areas that produce feelings of joy and pleasure. These foods trick the brain into believing they are good, in much the same way the brain reacts to drug addiction.[65]

The soda and fast food industries grew alongside the rise of processed foods, and soon led to the supersized "value meal" cultures we know today. Fast-food companies saw the advantage of packaging their food products into "meals," offering larger portions of fries and sodas that were now much cheaper to produce, thus increasing their profit margin. By the 1980s soda became so cheap to produce in large part because of the creation of high-fructose corn syrup that made it economically feasible for companies to increase their drink sizes without added cost. The portions may have been bigger, but the nutritional content was far worse. A single can of cola, with its nine teaspoons of sugar, gave way to twenty-ounce bottles containing fifteen teaspoons of sugar and liter bottles with twenty-six teaspoons.[66]

Studies conducted on Indigenous peoples in the United States and Canada reveal the steady rise of obesity, correlating directly with the rise of market foods in their diets. For example, in the larger US population, obesity rates are also increasing, but for Native American adults and children, it is at a higher rate than that for all the other races combined.[67] This rapid rise in obesity among Native Americans has taken place in a very short period of time, over the last two generations, when more industrial processed foods became available along with a more sedentary lifestyle. During this time, processed foods made their way into Indigenous diets, becoming staple foods.[68] Which brings up an interesting point. In some cases, even what passes for Indigenous food is just more of the colonizer's diet. Take, for example, one of the most popular "Native" foods of all: frybread. Throughout the United States and Canada frybread has become engrained in Indigenous cultures, communities, and diets, and for some it is recognized as a traditional food. To this day frybread can be found at many Indigenous gatherings from powwows in the Plains states to Tribal Canoe Journeys on the Northwest Coast. It is made with flour, shortening, and salt and shaped and flattened into variously sized disks before being fried in grease or oil. Frybread is often called "Indian tacos," which are topped with ground meat, beans, cheese, lettuce, and sour cream, and it is also popular as a dessert, with variations including butter, powdered sugar, chocolate, honey, or syrup. *Health* magazine ranked frybread as one of the fifty fattiest foods in the United States.[69] Still, as Cherokee scholar Courtney Lewis discusses in her article "Frybread Wars," attacking Indigenous people for continuing to eat this unhealthy food challenges us to think about how it became central to Indigenous diets in the first place.[70] Our Indigenous history is one of removal, starvation, and forced reliance on federal commodity foods and ingredients like salt, sugar, flour, and dried milk. Not having access to traditional foods, many Indigenous people took what was available and created staples that allowed them to survive. "The creation of frybread," Lewis asserts, "is a part of an American Indian story of survival, and its value today is thus far greater than the sum of its ingredients."[71]

Of course, it is important to remember that Indigenous people are not one homogeneous group; they are diverse populations with their own subsistence activities, each with a wide range and variety of animals and plants that make up their traditional foods. As a result, the impact of industrial foods on Indigenous diets is also wide-ranging. Still, this does not obscure the plain fact that the chronic diseases that now kill most of us can be traced directly to the industrialization of our global food systems.[72] The medical community gives a lot of lip service to the importance of prevention and limiting processed foods, but the health-care industry makes huge profits from the new drugs and medical procedures to treat these chronic diseases.[73] As Michael Pollan asserts, "Medicine is learning how to keep alive the people whom the Western diet is making sick."[74]

The Journey to Health, Healing, and Wellness

I invite you to jump into my canoe as I take you on a journey of health, healing, and wellness by sharing stories, theories, and cultural understanding of our foodways. Join me and my Tseshaht community in our canoe and let us take you on a journey, paddling through colonial-driven waves of pain and sorrow but finding our way as we navigate through waves of hope and possibility, searching for the currents that lead us to healthy and strong cultures. Our canoe is reinforced with Nuu-chah-nulth principles of ʔiisaak, being respectful, and ʔuʔaałuk, taking care of, providing us with the ontological tools to reinforce, revitalize, and restore our healthy relationships to the plants, animals, lands, and waters that have provided us with spiritual sustenance and cultural strength and wellness—to understand our philosophy of ḥačatakma čawaak, everything is interconnected.

In the following chapter, through personal stories and stories shared with me over the years, I examine the importance of enacting food sovereignty and why having the right to eat our cultural and healthy foods, to define our food systems, and to have access to our traditional territories to harvest them, is fundamental to our tiičʕaqƛ, holistic health, and our cultural survival. In chapter 2, I discuss the relationship Northwest Coast Indigenous peoples have with salmon, which is central to and has shaped our cultural identity. I focus my attention on my Tseshaht community and how this traditional food was and still is the foundation of our culture, remaining an important staple food in our diets, and at the heart of our stories and shared experiences. In chapter 3, our canoe brings us to the Tseshaht Community Garden, a project created by my sister Gail Williams Gus to empower community members to live healthy lives and improve the individual and collective health of our community. The garden was cultivated on a former boarding school site, a school where many Tseshaht children suffered extreme physical, sexual, and emotional abuse. The purpose for growing a garden on lands scorched by colonial violence was to restore a healthy relationship with the nisma, land, and to create a place of healing for former students who relived these horrors every time they came to this site. While Gail's garden does not grow haʔum, traditional food, it is central to Tseshaht decolonization and self-determination through restoring community health and wellness and rebuilding a vibrant, healthy and sustainable nation.

We end our canoe journey at the home of kamâmakskwew waakiituusiis Nitanis Desjarlais and ńaasʔałuk John Rampanen, who made a concerted effort

I.1 Aunty Misbun picking qaałqaawi, wild blackberries. *Photograph courtesy of Melanie Braker.*

to decolonize their diets by moving their family to a remote area on Vancouver Island to live the way of their ancestors by harvesting and eating traditional foods. Finally, in the epilogue I look at how the global pandemic affected all of these stories—and how we can find a way forward in these challenging times.

Now I Understand Why My Aunty Misbun Said We Were "Bonding"

It was not until many years after I started my research on Indigenous food traditions that I began to reflect back on what my Aunty Misbun said when we were out picking qaałqaawi, wild blackberries, and what she meant when she said we were "bonding." She intuitively understood how our berry-picking tradition maintained and reinforced our bonds to our qaałqaawi relatives, our bonds to the nisma where they grew, and most important, our bond to each other—reinforcing the love between an aunt and her niece. When I began my research for this book, my aunty was very excited that I was going to include berry-picking stories. I told her I was really disappointed that we did not take photos while we were out on our berry-picking adventures and that I would love to have some photos in my book. I had hoped to go picking berries with her and get some photos, but my summer teaching schedule usually kept me from returning home when the qaałqaawi were ripened and ready. So in the summer of 2012, Aunty Misbun called my cousin Melanie and invited her to go. "She was so insistent we go out," Melanie laughs, "because we needed to get photos for your book."[75] So on a hot summer afternoon Melanie and Aunty Misbun got in their vehicle and headed out to find some qaałqaawi, checking the places that were known as good berry-picking sites. They made their way along one of the gravel roads until they finally came to a nice ṅačyuu, berry patch. My aunt grabbed her pails and headed out into the berry patch. In a short period of time she filled up her containers. She grabbed both her pails, which were brimming over with ripe, glistening qaałqaawi, and turned to Melanie and said, "Take some photos of me holding my berries. These photos are going to be awesome in Charlotte's book." And, teasingly, she said, "We're going to be famous." Melanie snapped photos of Aunty Misbun as she proudly posed with her arms wrapped around her bounty.[76] I never got the opportunity to pick qaałqaawi with my aunty again. The following year, succumbing to cancer, Aunty Misbun passed away.

tiičʕaqƛ

Understanding Food Sovereignty and Its Potential
for Indigenous Health and Decolonization

T O BEGIN this chapter on food sovereignty I share a story about my family and our tradition of picking qaałqaawi, trailing blackberries, to help understand its correlation with tiičʕaqƛ, holistic health, and decolonization, and for creating spaces where our food traditions are centralized and self-determined. As mentioned in the previous chapter, picking qaałqaawi was one of my favorite activities as a young girl and I have continued this tradition throughout my life. I have many wonderful stories about berry picking. I was raised in the berry-picking tradition, and each summer my family would gather together in a caravan of vehicles and head to the mountains in search of the delectable qaałqaawi. My grandpa, Hughie Watts, was the berry-picking location specialist and always knew where to find the most and best ńačyuu, or berry patch. As I also discussed in my opening chapter, colonization and removal led to the loss of many of our traditional harvesting sites, and many of these lands then fell under the control of forestry companies, which, through a slash-and-burn technique, engineered the lands for timber production. Still, my grandfather knew how to turn this settler-colonial desecration to his advantage. Having been raised with

traditional ecological knowledge of land burning, he knew that these areas that
were cleared to remove logs were also ideal places for wild blackberry growth.
Grandpa would drive through our former harvesting sites and when he saw the
areas that had been burned by forest companies, he would tell us, "In a couple
of years this is going to be a great spot to pick berries." And sure enough, it was.

When the qaałqaawi season arrived, my grandpa and other family members
would get the vehicles ready and gather all of us together to begin our journey
into the mountains where the qaałqaawi grew. We would pack our food and
water for the day and grab our berry-picking containers. We no longer utilized
the beautiful cedar-woven baskets that were used by our ancestors for picking
berries. Instead, we found new and innovative containers brought to our communities by settler society in the form of metal pots and plastic ice cream containers. When I was young, the main type of berry-picking container was a metal
cooking pot, which changed to plastic Tupperware bowls, and then eventually
we began using the Neapolitan ice cream 128-ounce circular plastic container,
which was ideal with its lid and handle. I am not an ice cream lover, but when
my mom brought it home, I devoured that ice cream until I got brain freeze, just
so that I could have this container for picking! I cannot tell you how much this
container transformed the way young kids picked qaałqaawi. The number one
issue we had when we were trekking up and down the mountains was spilling
our berries. There is nothing worse than when you fill your container, only to
have all its delicious contents spill out before you can make your way back to
the vehicle to transfer the berries into the larger bins. But sometimes those flimsy
containers with no tops worked to our advantage. Occasionally, we kids would
get a little carried away when we were picking and more berries ended up in
our mouths than in our containers. When we got back to the vehicle to transfer
our berries into the larger pots, my grandparents would see that we only had a
few berries. We would put on our saddest faces and tell them about our "mis-
haps" and how we fell and spilled most of them. My grandpa would look at us
with a stern face and say, "You need to be more careful next time." And then he
would turn away, and we could see a slight flicker of a smile on his face because
he knew we were fibbing; the giveaway—the deep red stains on our lips and
tongues. We could never pull anything over on our grandpa.

The drive up the mountains could take anywhere from one to several hours,
depending on where my grandpa chose to look first or where there had been
slash burning the year before. We would make our way up the windy, dusty

roads with kids either in the back of the trucks or squished in the back seats of the cars, happy with anticipation and excitement for our next berry-picking adventure. Many times, as we were driving along the mountain roads, we would run into other community members who were also out for a day of berry picking. And we would usually run into my grandpa's sister Agnes Sam, or Green Aunty, as she was also known,[1] who shared the love of berry picking and would also be out with her family looking for the ultimate qaałqaawi ńačyuu, blackberry patch.

Never, Ever Reveal Your ńačyuu!

We would pull up beside Green Aunty's vehicle driven by one of her sons, and with her younger children and grandchildren crammed in the back seat. My grandpa would roll down his window and say to his sister, "Did you find any berries on that mountain?" pointing to a mountain nearby. Green Aunty would reply, "No, nothing on that mountain." They would chat for a little longer, tell a few stories, laugh, catch up on the local community gossip, and then we would drive away. As soon as Green Aunty was out of sight my grandpa would head his vehicle straight up that very mountain where Green Aunty said there were no qaałqaawi. My grandpa knew his sister was lying because he would tell her the exact same story when she asked him if he had found any good ńačyuu. And we were sworn to secrecy and told never to reveal where a good berry patch was, and we would keep this secret even when Green Aunty or any of our other relatives would try to get us to spill the beans. My grandpa and his sister loved each other dearly, but we all grew up with this family rule that we still keep today: Never, ever reveal your ńačyuu!

When Grandpa would find the perfect ńačyuu we would pile out of our caravan of vehicles and head up the mountain following the narrow, grassy paths, spreading out across the landscape in search of berry vines. Once we found a good patch, we would take out our containers and get ready for hours of picking. Every so often we would stand up and stretch out our backs, see how our other relatives were doing, and compare our picking accomplishments. We would scan the mountainside for my grandpa, who was always easy to find because he loved to wear a white cap on his head, which clearly stood out among the blankets of green trees and bushes, even if he was on another mountain slope. He, too, was keeping track of us, making sure we were safe but, most of all, making sure we young ones were picking berries and not horsing around.

My grandma, Grace, always got first dibs on the qaałqaawi that were growing close to the road where we parked our vehicles, and she would shoo us younger ones away and tell us to go farther up the mountain path to pick. One afternoon my cousin Daryl and I were walking back to the vehicle to transfer the berries from our small container into the larger ones that were in the trunk. As we were nearing the road, we saw our grandma hunched over behind a fallen tree, picking berries from the vines growing along the stump. On the other side of the tree stump was a black bear eating berries from the same vine. Trying to stay calm we inched closer to Grandma, trying not to startle the bear. When we were near enough, we said to her softly, "Grandma, there's a bear on the other side of the stump." My grandma replied, "I know. I see her. Leave her alone. She loves the berries too." And my grandma just kept on picking.

After a couple of hours of picking qaałqaawi, we would all meet back at the vehicles, take out the foods and beverages we had packed, and sit down for a meal, typically salmon sandwiches and usually Tang (obviously not a traditional food, but it was the big drink back in the 1970s). While eating, the adults would catch up with each other, sharing stories in a familial exchange of love and laughter. Once we completed our meal, we would head back up the mountain paths to continue picking berries. On a good day of picking we would average about five gallons of berries. When all of the large containers in the vehicles were filled, we called it a day and began our drive down the mountainside headed toward home to begin processing the qaałqaawi. Sometimes, if it was not too late and if we were driving past Sproat or Great Central Lake on our way home, Grandpa and the other adults driving in our family caravan would stop the vehicles so that we kids could go for a quick dip. We especially loved this on a particularly hot and dry day; it was so refreshing to jump into the cool water. My grandpa did this as a way to show his appreciation for the work we did in contributing berries to our communal pots. But I also think he and the other adults knew this would be a great way to get the dust and dirt off us before we got back to my grandparents' home.

When we arrived back at my grandparents' home, my grandma, my mom, and my aunties would divide the berries and get them ready to process. This usually meant canning them, a process that involves cleaning off all the stems, small sticks, and other debris, washing the berries in cold water, then placing them in jars. Pectin and a little sugar or honey may be added for taste. The jars are then sealed with lids and rings and placed in a large canner that is filled with hot water up to an inch from the top of the jars in the bottom row. A lid is placed on the canner and the water is brought to a boil. The cooking time is short, ten to fifteen minutes. Once cooked, the jars are removed and placed on a table until they cool down. Once cooled, they can be stored away for future use. Or, sometimes, we would just put the berries in plastic bags and freeze them. My grandparents would keep a larger share for when we would get together for our large family dinners at their house. And some berries were always put aside for my grandma to make her delicious blackberry dumplings (a recipe I wish I remembered!), which she would make for that evening's dinner. We would all gather around the table, sharing our berry-picking stories as we ate one of our delicious traditional foods.

The Northwest Coast—Land of Salmon and Cedar

My Nuu-chah-nulth community of Tseshaht is situated within the larger area defined as the Northwest Coast, extending over 1,400 miles and encompassing the jagged coastlines of southeastern Alaska, British Columbia, Washington and Oregon states, and Northern California. It is an area characterized as the "land of salmon and cedar," and was the home of some of the most diverse and richest Indigenous cultures in the world, nations that flourished in abundances of marine mammals and dense vegetation in an area with mild winters and wet summers.[2] The waterways provided us with an abundance of food, and the rainforest, populated by western red and yellow cedar, provided us with an impressive material culture. We fished primarily for salmon, but also harvested other local fish, sea mammals, and shellfish, and in the case of my people, the Nuu-chah-nulth, and our relatives the Makah in Washington State, we hunted whales. Land animals such as deer, elk, and mountain goat were also hunted.

Biological diversity created an abundance of foods along the Northwest Coast, which we and other Coastal Nations harvested by fishing, hunting, gathering, and cultivating plants and medicines. The harvesting, cultivation, preparation, sharing, and trading of our foods was conducted within our pre-scribed cultural values based on respect, reciprocity, interdependency, and eco-logical sustainability. Our food systems functioned in healthy interdependent relationships with our environment and were maintained through the active participation in traditional land and food systems.³ The kinds and quantities of foods that were available to us were dependent on keeping this symbiotic relationship strong and healthy, and resources were maintained through the transfer of traditional ecological knowledge monitoring the environmental health and species diversity, as stewards and protectors. As a result, our traditional foodways are enmeshed in the ecosystems in which we thrive.

When I was growing up a good portion of my daily diet consisted of haʔum, or traditional food, and we frequently ate salmon, halibut, herring eggs, and seafood as well as deer and moose meat and a variety of berries and plants, which we harvested and processed. I was raised on very healthy foods, eating salmon or seafood three or four times a week, accompanied by wild berries as well as fruit from the orchard behind my grandparent's home that was planted by the Indian agents in the late 1800s, when they were attempting to make us into farmers. So how did we get to this place of unhealthiness? As an Indigenous food studies scholar born and raised in my Nuu-chah-nulth community of Tseshaht I have studied, witnessed, and experienced how colonization, the ongoing impacts of settler colonialism, boarding schools, habitat destruction, socioeconomic marginalization, and the imposition of a Western diet have impacted my people's physical, nutritional, and spiritual health and caused us and Indigenous peoples globally to be food insecure.

Food Sovereignty and the Centrality of qaałqaawi to Tseshaht Culture

Food sovereignty has been defined as "the right of peoples to healthy and culturally appropriate food produced through ecologically sound and sustainable methods."⁴ Beyond nutritional health, Indigenous food sovereignty reinforces familial and social bonds of generosity and reciprocity in harvesting, sharing, and eating our food while also decreasing our dependence on processed foods. I have witnessed this firsthand. Our berry-picking tradition united my family and strengthened our social and ancestral relationships to one another while reaffirming our physical relationships to the qaałqaawi, to other plants and animals we came in contact with while harvesting, and to the lands, soil, air, and water that provided this nutritious and wholesome source of food. Within these mutual and symbiotic relationships of respect and reciprocity, my family was enacting food sovereignty.

In the pre-contact and early contact periods, in my Tseshaht community, berry picking and gathering roots and camas were considered a women's economic activity. Men's activities were harvesting fish and seafood as well as hunting deer and elk. While many studies of Northwest Coast Indigenous economies focus on males as the main food providers through fishing and hunting activities, women's roles as berry and root harvesters were equally important and contributed just as much to the dietary health of our communities. For my community, we ate many different varieties of berries, but qaałqaawi were central to our diet and significant to our health, having a high nutritional value with lots of dietary fiber, vitamin C, vitamin K, folic acid, vitamin B, and the essential mineral manganese.[5]

Prior to colonization, when our hereditary chiefdom system was strong, our hawiih (chiefs) had stewardship over the hahuułi, or ancestral homelands, and would oversee the economic resources and activities of their ʔuuštaqimł, family or lineage group, and masčim, community members, including the root-digging and berry-picking sites, which were part of their tupaati, or hereditary prerogative.[6] The hawiih had clearly defined tangible and intangible rights to lands, waterways, plants, and animals as well as to names, songs, dances, and ceremonies that were acknowledged and that were affirmed in our Potlatch system. An important feature of these rights was understanding the responsibilities that came with them, especially in treating all living things within his hahuułi with the utmost respect and reverence so that a relationship based on reciprocity would be upheld and reinforced. Thus the word hahuułi meant more than just a right of ownership, as explained by Nuu-chah-nulth elder Roy Haiyupis:

> [hahuułi] indicates . . . that the hereditary chiefs have the responsibility to take care of the forests, the land and the sea within his [hahuułi], and a responsibility to look after his [masčim], or tribal members. . . . Embedded within the [hahuułi] initiated from [the chief's] rights to ownership of tribal territories, lies the key to the social and cultural practices, tribal membership and property ownership—economic, environmental and resource controls to . . . sustain life for the tribe today and for generations to come.[7]

Nuu-chah-nulth-aht,[8] and other Indigenous peoples, have a belief that all things in our natural world have spirits, which we recognize through ceremony.

First Species and First Foods ceremonies were conducted to honor them for gift-ing themselves as food, eliciting a relationship based on reciprocity and a sense of sacredness and gratitude attached to the spirit of a plant or animal that gives itself to humans. These are what Robin Kimmerer calls "cultures of reciprocity," where humans and other living things exist in an interconnected world in which all are equally worthy of respect.[9]

The ḥawiiḥ had clearly defined areas that they protected, managed, and cared for. Berry-picking sites were clearly marked with cedar stakes driven into the ground to serve as boundaries for the berry patches and to let others know that these harvesting areas were under the stewardship of a particular chief. When the berries were ripe the chief would have first claim to the ńačyuu, or berry patch, and women within his ʔuuštaqimł would be sent to gather the berries for him. The harvesting of plants, roots, and berries would begin in late spring with salmonberry shoots, which we call ṁaayi, one of my favorite tradi-tional foods when I was growing up. It has a delicious sweet taste, and you eat it by peeling back the outer skin to reveal a soft and crunchy inner shoot. Many community members still pick and eat ṁaayi, but like our other traditional foods, it now competes with store-bought sweet foods and candy.

By early summer the berry crops would start to ripen and the women would take their baskets made of woven cedar bark, which they carried on their backs secured with a strap over the forehead or chest. They would paddle their canoes, travelling along the waterways collecting berries, along with roots and plants, emptying their baskets into large boxes in the canoe as they paddled along the shores."[10] They would leave their villages for several days as they travelled through the territory, making temporary bark shelters in the places they stopped to sleep. After they had enough berries for the winter months, they would return to the village to begin processing them. Some berries would be eaten immedi-ately, but most of them would be preserved by spreading them out on planks and then pressing the planks together for drying the berries. Once they were dried, the berries would be stored in baskets until eaten, traded, or fed or gifted to guests at Potlatch ceremonies. The first qaałqaawi harvest would be welcomed through a feast held by the chief to pay respect to the berry plant that provided this food, to acknowledge and show gratitude to the women who picked the berries, and to share his bounty with community members and other guests who were invited to his Potlatch. Berries would be eaten with an accompaniment of whale or seal oil.[11]

Berries were also significant to the Indigenous trade economy that developed along the Northwest Coast. Once berries and other plant foods were processed and preserved, the chiefs would trade them through this network, thus distributing foods to areas that may have had scarcity while also increasing the chief's importance and wealth. In the early contact period, non-Indigenous explorers, traders, missionaries, and settlers also received berries through the food trade. In some cases, receiving these nutritious foods meant the difference between starvation and survival for them.[12]

Understanding Food Sovereignty

In 1993 peasants, small-scale farmers, and Indigenous communities organized into a global agrarian movement, La Via Campesina, representing 148 organizations from sixty-nine countries, forming the strongest voice yet in radical opposition to what they described as a "globalized, neoliberal model of agricultural food production." The movement linked the growing food, economic, and environmental crises to the continued growth of an industrial, capital-intensive, and corporate-led model of agriculture. Created by destructive economic policies that marginalized small-scale farmers at the expense of multinational corporations, the model called for the removal of farmers from their land and forced them into the global market economy as wage laborers.[13]

In a conference held in 1996 in Tlaxcala, Mexico, La Via Campesina criticized the state-led food security movement to end global hunger.[14] This food security program, they asserted, did little to address the real issue, the control over food production and distribution. Via Campesina also argued that the current regime continued to promote agricultural practices that benefitted transnational corporations and undermined small-scale farmers.[15] The Tlaxcala conference introduced a new concept, "food sovereignty," and established eleven principles that were integrated into La Via Campesina's Position on Food Sovereignty, presented at the World Food Summit in Rome in November 1996.

The World Food Summit brought together representatives from 185 countries and the European Community with close to ten thousand participants, who debated one of the most important issues facing the planet: the eradication of hunger. In the NGO Response to the Rome Declaration on World Food Security a six-point plan was presented, which relied on a rights-based discourse that challenged transnational capitalist control over the globalized food market and proposed a new framework for ending global hunger:

> We propose a new model for achieving food security that calls into question many of the existing assumptions, policies and practices. This model, based on decentralization, challenges the current model, based on a concentration of wealth and power, which now threatens global food security, cultural diversity, and the very ecosystems that sustain life on the planet. . . . Each nation must have the right to food sovereignty to achieve the level of food sufficiency and nutritional quality it considers appropriate without suffering retaliation of any kind.[16]

The definition of food sovereignty was further developed in various forums and meetings. The Nyéléni International Forum for Food Sovereignty, held in Sélingué, Mali, in 2007, brought together five hundred delegates from various organizations in eighty countries to address the need for an international plan for resistance. They agreed that the plan would need to support political autonomy and privilege the rights and interests of local producers, distributors, and consumers. Together, they concluded, these stakeholders could establish a decision-making process to alleviate hunger and food insecurity. The Nyéléni Declaration articulated what is now the most-cited definition of food sovereignty:

> Food sovereignty is the right of peoples to healthy and culturally appropriate food produced through ecologically sound and sustainable methods, and their right to define their own food and agricultural systems. It puts the aspirations and needs of those who produce, distribute and consume food at the heart of food systems and policies rather that the demands of markets and corporations.[17]

The concept of food sovereignty was framed within a larger rights discourse and the ability for all people to produce their own foods freely and independently in a political framework that recognized territorial autonomy. Food sovereignty, the delegates stressed, could only operate in a world where political sovereignty of all peoples was recognized.[18] This emerging food sovereignty movement challenged the hegemony of transnational capital in the food system, articulating the need to stop viewing food as a "commodity," and asserting that the political rights to produce and distribute food be returned to the producers and consumers.[19]

This notion of food sovereignty became a uniting call to small-scale farmers and Indigenous peoples throughout the world. While this movement developed in an agrarian-based, Latin American context,[20] Indigenous peoples with fishing, hunting, and gathering traditions were able to connect to its underlying philosophy that all nations, including Indigenous Nations, have the right to define strategies and policies and develop food systems and practices that reflect their own cultural values around producing, consuming, and distributing food.

Indigenizing Food Sovereignty

In the mid-1990s Indigenous peoples in Canada and the United States began exploring ways in which food sovereignty could be employed as a concept to create dialogue and action around the revitalization of Indigenous food practices and ecological knowledge. The Working Group on Indigenous Food Sovereignty (WGIFS) was created in 2006 and was one of the first Indigenous groups in Canada to explore the new concept of food sovereignty. Through its participation with the British Columbia Food Systems Network (BCFSN), the WGIFS began to articulate ways food sovereignty could be defined and applied in order to address pressing issues facing Indigenous communities as they responded to their own health needs.[21] Coming together in meetings, conferences, and discussion groups, Indigenous elders, traditional harvesters, and community members redefined food sovereignty by moving it beyond a "rights-based" discourse and centering it in Indigenous foods and ecological knowledge, which emphasized ancestral values and wisdom.[22]

The WGIFS developed four key principles of Indigenous food sovereignty that Indigenous peoples and communities could use as a framework as they addressed their food needs. (1) Sacred sovereignty: food is a sacred gift from the Creator. (2) Participatory: this is a call to action, whereby people have a responsibility to uphold and nurture healthy and interdependent relationships with the ecosystem that provides the land, water, plants, and animals as food. (3) Self-determination: food sovereignty needs to be placed within a context of Indigenous self-determination with the freedom and ability to respond to community needs around food. (4) Policy: it provides a restorative framework for reconciling Indigenous food and cultural values with colonial laws and policies.[23]

Enacting Indigenous food sovereignty requires peeling away the layers of colonialism that have been the Indigenous lived experience and redefining our lives within our own philosophical and ancestral teachings and wisdom. At the same time, Indigenous communities are distinct and unique, making it impossible to define food sovereignty in a way that reflects all of our realities. Still, as WGIFS director Dawn Morrison points out, we Indigenous peoples are united by eco-philosophical principles that have guided our interactions with the environment and the nonhuman world and have informed our food systems.[24]

In the next sections I discuss four themes: building relationships and affirming responsibilities; restorative food justice; fostering health and well-being; and strengthening social, familial, and community bonds. These themes intersect with and build on the WGIFS four principles that I feel help contextualize Indigenous food sovereignty and situate it within the decolonial struggles taking place in our communities today.

Building Relationships and Affirming Responsibilities

As I stated earlier, the concept of food sovereignty was framed within a larger rights discourse, that being the right of peoples to healthy and culturally appropriate food, and the right to define their own food and agricultural systems freely and independently. Having the political and cultural right to your traditional foods recognized by governments through policy, as the WGIFS has identified, can provide a framework for reconciling Indigenous food and cultural values with colonial laws and policies. This would align with and support the rights contained in the United Nations Declaration on the Rights of Indigenous Peoples (UNDRIP), and more specifically with Article 20, which states, "Indigenous peoples have the right to maintain and develop their political, economic and social systems or institutions, to be secure in the enjoyment of their own means of subsistence and development, and to engage freely in all their traditional and other economic activities."[25] In 2016 Canada took some legal steps and endorsed the document as part of the movement toward reconciliation with Indigenous peoples, but it has not officially adopted the UNDRIP into law.[26] In 2019 British Columbia and the Northwest Territories went further and made a political move to write the UNDRIP into their provincial and territorial laws.[27]

In looking at Indigenous food sovereignty through a "rights-based" lens, scholars such as Jeff Corntassel (Cherokee) argue that "the existing rights discourse can only take Indigenous peoples so far" through its emphasis on state political and legal recognition of Indigenous rights. Rather than focus on achieving political and legal recognition of the right to food sovereignty, Corntassel turns the attention toward Indigenous community action in emphasizing the cultural responsibilities and relationships Indigenous peoples have with the land, water, plants, and animals that have sustained their cultures.[28]

Placed within the concept of self-determination as defined in the WGIFS principles, Indigenous food sovereignty aligns with principles developed by Corntassel's notion of "sustainable self-determination," which positions responsibilities and relationships at the core of Indigenous self-determination. In order to decolonize, Indigenous peoples need to direct change from within and through action, change, strategies, and policies in working toward becoming sustainable self-determining nations.[29] Indigenizing food sovereignty places emphasis on Indigenous responsibility, mutuality, kinship, and relationships with the natural world; a world, as Kimmerer contends, that is built on reciprocity between humans and nonhumans, creating duties and responsibilities for both: "Just as all beings have a duty to me, I have a duty to them," Kimmerer writes. "If an animal gives its life to feed me, I am in turn bound to support its life. If I receive a stream's gift of pure water, then I am responsible for returning a gift in kind. An integral part of a human's education is to know those duties and how to perform them."[30] Embedded within Indigenous eco-philosophy and worldview is the cultural knowledge and understanding that people, animals, land, water, and air are interconnected in a web of life that emphasizes good relationships based on gratitude and respect. Indigenous food sovereignty, therefore, embodies a deep spiritual appreciation for food as a sacred gift. Understanding our traditional foods in this way, Morrison says, keeps "foods alive spiritually" and is recognized in rituals, offerings, and ceremonies.[31]

Restorative Food Justice

Indigenous food sovereignty entails a rebuilding of the relationships between humans and nonhumans in a restorative framework. The human-ecosystem relationship is characterized as one of reciprocity and respect, where humans do not control nature but live in harmony with it. Thus restoring the health of Indigenous communities requires restoring the health of the land. Or, as Kimmerer so aptly states, "We restore the land and the land restores us."[32] In his book *Eating the Landscape*, Indigenous ethnobotanist Enrique Salmón weaves his historical and cultural knowledge into a tapestry of understanding Indigenous environmental stewardship and the ancestral relationship Indigenous peoples have to the world around them.

> The knowledge I learned from my family was one aspect of a trove of culturally accumulated ecological knowledge. When they introduced me to individual plants, they also introduced my kinship to the plants and to the land from where they and we emerged. They were introducing me to my relatives. Through this way of knowing, especially with regard to kinship, I realized a comfort and a sense of security that I was bound to everything around me in a reciprocal relationship.[33]

Indigenous food sovereignty is defined within a restorative context, one that works to nurture individual and community health by repairing and fostering these healthy relationships. In the Indigenous worldview a healthy landscape sustains humans and nonhumans in what Kimmerer characterizes as "circles of reciprocity." Hence rebuilding and restoring sustainable and healthy relationships between humans and nonhumans through food sovereignty is not only good medicine for each; it is, as Kimmerer states, "medicine for the earth."[34] Within Indigenous cosmologies, scholars Sam Grey and Raj Patel assert, both landscapes and foodscapes occupy a simultaneously physical, spiritual, and social geography:

> Just as kinship is not restricted to consanguine human beings, sacredness does not merely congeal in particular places, but is a quality of the totality of the natural world—including all of the life-forms that provide sustenance and frame trade networks. Thus, food can be seen as the most direct manifestation of the relationships between Indigenous peoples and homelands, and it consequently occupies a central space in traditional thought.[35]

The Indigenous food sovereignty movement embodies a decolonization framework and through action and practice seeks to heal the wounds of colonialism and repair our relationships to the natural world. Throughout his life,

Salmón's identity was grounded in what he calls "an encoded library of cultural and ecological knowledge" that united his relatives through the foods they ate and the recipes they shared, connecting them to the landscape in a familial relationship of respect.[36] For Indigenous peoples, our health and well-being are tied to our ancestral lands, to the waters, and to the plants and animals. In order to return to healthy communities, we need to restore healthy relationships to our ecosystems, which requires having access to our lands and waters, where we harvested, fished, and hunted. Our foods and ecological knowledge are embedded in our land and seascapes. The land and the food that comes from it are our source of knowledge and history. As Salmón asserts, "the food and the land where it grows remain the source of cultural memory."[37]

Fostering Health and Well-Being

Within the history of Indigenous peoples, colonization plays a key role in determining poor health through its disruption of our healthy relationships with our ecosystems, traditional foodways, and transfer of ecological and ancestral knowledge. Colonial policies such as the boarding schools weakened cultural practices and broke down our languages, creating disconnection from our cultural identity. Even for those not in the schools, colonialism maintained perpetual marginalization, leading to lack of autonomy and self-esteem, exacerbating the health disparities we see in our Indigenous communities today.[38]

As discussed in the introduction to this book, the industrialization of foods globally and the rise of processed food have created food insecurity throughout the world. For Indigenous peoples with place-based food economies, our food insecurity has reached epidemic levels with heart disease, diabetes, autoimmune disease, and others rising at alarming rates, making a return to our subsistence economies crucial to our cultural survival.[39] But what does it mean to be healthy?

Indigenous health has physical, emotional, psychological, and spiritual aspects that work together to heal and protect from disease through traditional foodways and ecosystems that maintain them. Being "healthy" is more than just our physical well-being; it means being spiritually and emotionally healthy—feeding our bodies with traditional and healthy foods and feeding our minds and spirits with our cultural teachings. For Indigenous people, our physical, spiritual, and emotional health is directly related to our ability to eat our traditional foods.[40] Restoring our traditional food practices allows us to experience a special connection to our cultures and our lands because every plant and animal carries its own spiritual gifts, and thus there is "a sense of vitality and belonging" that comes with eating the foods that provided our ancestors with optimum health and longevity.[41]

The Inuit in northern Alaska have a saying: "I am what I am because of what I eat."[42] Studies of the Indigenous whaling nations in the Arctic demonstrate how traditional foods, especially whales, are more than just nutritional sustenance; they have social, cultural, spiritual, and psychological significance as well. While a high value is placed on whales as a healthy food source, the tradition of whaling maintains community solidarity and collective security through the communal hunts and the processing, distributing, and consuming of whale products by the community members. Whaling serves to link the Inuit materially, symbolically, and spiritually to their cultural heritage and ancestral knowledge.[43]

As Indigenous people, we have an emotional connection to our traditional foods and see them as impacting our physical and nutritional well-being and having strong cultural and social values. There is a delicate balance between nutrition, emotional health, and social contact through complex interactions between people, brain chemistry, and the foods being eaten.[44] Eating traditional healthy foods turns on our neurotransmitters that release what are referred to as "happy chemicals": dopamine, endorphins, oxytocin, and serotonin, which send messages to the brain that make us feel joyful and content.[45] Many studies have been conducted with Indigenous peoples in northern Canada and Alaska to examine cultural and dietary change resulting from an increase in industrialized and processed foods. These communities have stayed connected to their traditional harvesting practices even with the increase in market and processed foods. Studies showed that even though these store-bought foods were available, traditional foods still retained their cultural and social importance and were associated with good feelings, health, and pleasurable events, especially when the foods were harvested. Similarly, a study conducted with the Yukon First Nations, Dene/Métis and Inuit women in Canada's Arctic communities between 1993 and 2003, included the question, "What do you think are the most important advantages of traditional food?" Women in these communities responded, "traditional food is healthy," "[traditional food] has more iron," and "[traditional food] makes your blood strong."[46] When asked what the socio-political benefits were of eating traditional foods the respondents remarked, "keeps our tradition," "brings people together," and "involves family in food prep[aration]."[47]

Strengthening Social, Familial, and Community Bonds

As I reflect back on berry picking with my relatives, I realized as I got older how important this tradition was to maintaining and strengthening the social and cultural bonds among us. I grew up in a large, tight-knit family. My mother was one of eleven siblings, who all grew up in close geographic proximity to each other. I was raised next door to my grandparents and they, along with my aunts and uncles, my mother's sisters and brothers, shared in the upbringing of their grandchildren. Our haʔum and traditions of berry picking and salmon fishing are important in reinforcing social and familial ties. The harvesting, processing, and sharing of qaaɫqaawi created a space where our elders transferred their cultural and foods knowledge to us younger ones, reaffirming our cultural identity as Tseshaht while strengthening our relationships and connections to our traditional lands, ecosystems, and the plants and animals where harvesting took place.

As we are social creatures, our ability to function in healthy interdependent relationships is directly influenced by our ability to maintain balance and harmony within our own bodies. In turn, our ability to maintain healthy bodies is directly influenced by the emotions we experience in positive social interactions. Working with family and community members to hunt, fish, gather, or prepare Indigenous foods can increase mental and emotional health through bonding and creating memories that can help build or enhance relationships.[48] In *Eating the Landscape*, Enrique Salmón connects his Rarámuri (Tarahumara) identity to his family's tradition of eating and sharing tamales, one of their traditional foods:

> My reaffirmation of identity and connection to place is not a direct result of the tamales, but come more from the processes that surround tamales, beans, raisins inside tamales, and my grandmother's herbal teas. The processes interconnect family, landscape, collection knowledge, all of which sustain and revitalize a sense of self and place. . . . I am eating the memories and knowledge associated with those foods. The elements of the stories, the jokes, and the intricate contextualized experience become embedded every time the eating

takes place. It becomes a form of mimetic regeneration to eat one's family's recipes.[49]

In the summer of 2015 I held a luncheon at our Tseshaht Administration Building and invited community members to come and share a meal with me while sharing their food tradition stories. Many of the stories about our haʔum focused on salmon, with salmon remaining one of the central traditional foods in our diets. Most of our community members continue to fish and process salmon, which I discuss in the next chapter. However, not too many people in my community still pick qaałqaawi on a regular or annual basis anymore, and as the community members shared with me, it was not because they or their relatives lost the taste for these berries. There were other factors, mainly economic ones, that kept them from exercising this tradition. In most Tseshaht families, the husband and wife worked, and they could not afford to take a couple of days off work to pick berries, or were too tired after a week of working to gather their families together to pick berries during the weekends. With other community members, it was just not having the economic resources for gas and vehicles to travel long distances to the berry harvesting sites in the mountains. Some community members did share family berry-picking stories, but these were usually in the past tense, stories from their childhood.

Integral to coastal Indigenous people's cultures is the social gathering or feast known as the Potlatch.[50] The word Potlatch comes from the Chinook trade language and was derived from the Nuu-chah-nulth word, p̓ačiƛ, which means "to give." The Potlatch reflected and perpetuated Nuu-chah-nulth social organization, and in pre-contact times only the ḥaw̓iiḥ or chiefs held Potlatches, which they used to announce, make a claim to, and validate the hereditary privileges or rights they acquired at birth. They were also used as a social mechanism to maintain harmony within their ʔuuštaqimł, family or lineage group, by acknowledging their skills and labor. The ḥaw̓ił (chief) and his family invited guests to witness the claim being made and assumed the role of host. The chief declared his intentions to the guests, and their acceptance and reciprocation in their Potlatches validated these claims to status and privilege. While the purpose of Potlatches was to pass on titles of rank and their associated privileges to designated heirs of the ḥaw̓iiḥ, they functioned also to distribute food surpluses and special local products to the people invited to witness the claim being made.[51] These foods and other items were given as gifts to the invited guests, whose acceptance of them acknowledged their acceptance of the claim being made.[52]

Today anyone in our community can host a Potlatch. They are still held to transfer and bestow names, to celebrate marriages, to recognize a youth's coming of age, and to mourn and recognize the death of a tribal member. The Potlatch continues to serve an important economic and social function through the sharing and distribution of food and material goods. Community member Darrell Ross Sr. shared a contemporary berry-picking story, one that connected this food tradition to our coastal Potlatch and to the social, family, and community bonding aspect of this tradition. In 1992 Darrell and his family were preparing for a Potlatch they were holding to name their three children and were gathering haʔum that they were going to share with their guests. One of the foods was qaaɬqaawi. In preparation, he and his family packed into their vehicles and headed to some of their favorite berry-picking areas and eventually found a huge n̓ačyuu, one that took them three days to pick. They harvested over five gallons of qaaɬqaawi, which they fed to their guests attending the Potlatch. Darrell says:

> It was my proudest moment. I felt so happy that we could share these berries with our guests and that gathering these berries was something that we did together as a family. This is the communal aspect of our foods, and the practice of feasting. Getting ready for this feast made me really understand this. These food gathering activities such as berry picking brought our families together.[53]

Darrell and many other community members connect our food traditions to ḥaaḥuupa, a traditional form of teaching to pass on knowledge, guidance, counsel, or advice. Throughout the years I have attended many feasts, gatherings, and Potlatches and listened to our elders talk about the importance of ḥaaḥuupa and passing down of knowledge through observance and stories. This, as Darrell explained, was central to social bonding and knowledge transfer while sharing a meal. He says, "In Nuu-chah-nulth culture there is a strong belief in mealtime ḥaaḥuupa and that you talk to your kids when you feed them. As they take in the food, they also take in what you are telling them, and they retain this knowledge. At mealtime you have their attention at the table."[54] Linda Thomas grew up picking berries and reflected on the social aspects of this tradition and the gathering together of their family to process the berries after a day of harvesting. She says, "We would pick berries in the morning and then start making the jam late at night when it cooled off. To think how our mothers and grandmothers all did this to teach us so that we understood this was our job. To this day, I have never forgotten these teachings."[55]

Indigenous Food Sovereignty Initiatives

Today many Indigenous communities throughout Canada and the United States are enacting food sovereignty as a way to reconnect to their traditional food sources, to restore and strengthen individual and community health and well-ness, and to assert their cultural and political autonomy. Traditional foods have become a potent cultural symbol as Indigenous peoples recognize that eating our traditional foods, and making the choice to eat these foods, is in itself a political act, a resistance to colonialism. It is central to decolonization and is an exercise in self-determination. Food sovereignty is intricately linked to cultural sovereignty, and as Ojibwe environmentalist, economist, and writer Winona LaDuke states, "You can't say you're sovereign if you can't feed yourself," a phrase shared with her by Oneida elder Paul "Sugar Bear" Smith.[56]

Indigenous food sovereignty initiatives continue to grow and expand upon foundational work from Anishinaabe environmental and food activist Winona LaDuke and others. LaDuke is the founding director of the White Earth Land Recovery Project (WELRP). WELRP was created in 1989 to recover ancestral lands of the White Earth Anishinaabeg lost through colonization and to return these lands to the stewardship of the White Earth tribal government. Central to this project were the revitalization of their language, reinstating traditional agricultural practices, restoration of their traditional corn seed stocks, and strengthening self-reliance and self-determination.[57] WELRP established one of the first seed-saving programs and libraries, creating a seed-saving movement that spread throughout the United States and Canada. They grow a variety of Indigenous corn seeds and share their seed growing information with other Indigenous communities who are seeking to create their own seed sovereignty projects and seed banks.[58]

Enriching the growing canon of Indigenous foods studies is the 2019 book *Indigenous Food Sovereignty in the United States: Restoring Cultural Knowledge, Protecting Environments, and Regaining Health,* which brings together Indigenous voices from US geographical regions ranging from Alaska, Hawaii, to the South-west, Southeast, Northwest, Great Plains, and California, articulating their understanding of food sovereignty and its potential for strengthening Indige-nous food traditions and restoring health and wellness in Indigenous communi-ties. The book was edited by Devon Mihesuah (Choctaw) and Elizabeth Hoover (Mohawk), two Indigenous scholars whose own academic and community-based work has created awareness of Indigenous food sovereignty. Both have played fundamental roles in the growing Indigenous foods movement. Mihesuah has written numerous publications on Indigenous health and wellness issues and manages the American Indian Health and Diet Project at the University of Kansas.[59] Hoover's teaching, research, and publications focus on environmental health and justice.[60] She created and manages the blog *From Garden Warriors to Good Seeds: Indigenizing the Local Food Movement*, and serves on the Native American Food Sovereignty Alliance (NAFSA) and the Slow Food Turtle Island Association.[61]

The essays Mihesuah and Hoover curate are written by Indigenous schol-ars, activists, and chefs who address important topics such as defining and enacting food sovereignty, restoring community health and wellness by strengthening traditional ecological knowledge, restoring seed banks, revi-talizing traditional ecosystems, and finding solutions to the issue of environ-mental degradation brought on by climate change. These personal stories demonstrate how Indigenous communities are distinct and unique, making it impossible to define food sovereignty in a way that reflects all Indigenous realities. Each contributor draws from a particular cultural background, his-tory, and set of traditions in sharing personal perspectives and insights into revitalizing and maintaining traditional foods systems and practices, restoring Indigenous individual and community health, and the challenges that arise in carrying out this work.[62]

In the Northwest Coast region the contemporary Indigenous foods movement emerged out of the foundational work by Indigenous people such as Valerie Segrest and Dawn Morrison. Segrest is an herbalist and nutrition educator and an enrolled member of the Muckleshoot Tribe in western Washington. In 2003 she and Elise Krohn, who is also an herbalist, native foods specialist, educator, and author, conducted research for the Traditional Foods of Puget Sound Proj-ect (2008–10), which explored the cultural significance of reviving traditional foodways as a way to improve individual, family, and community wellness.

This report led to the publication of their 2010 book, *Feeding the People, Feeding the Spirit: Revitalizing Northwest Coastal Indian Food Culture,* published by the Northwest Indian College, which is administered by the Lummi Nation in western Washington, and was connected to the college's Traditional Plants and Foods Program. Segrest and Krohn examine pre-contact coastal Indigenous food traditions, the disruption to these foodways as a result of colonization, the contemporary barriers to revitalizing food practices, and the revival of Indigenous food traditions as told through the voices, stories, and photos from the peoples of this region. The book includes important data on Northwest Coast plants and animals utilized as food by coastal Indigenous peoples, and provides delicious recipes that come from the heart of these communities.[63] Segrest has continued her important work with the Northwest Indian College's Traditional Plants and Foods Program and serves as coordinator of the Muckleshoot Food Sovereignty Project, where she teaches classes and holds workshops on Northwest Coast traditional foods.[64]

Dawn Morrison, mentioned earlier in this chapter, is the founder, chair, and coordinator of the Working Group on Indigenous Food Sovereignty (WGIFS) in British Columbia. Morrison is from the interior B.C. Secwepemc (Shuswap) community but has lived in Vancouver for over twenty years. Since 1983 Dawn has worked in horticulture, ethnobotany, adult education, and restoration of natural ecosystems. She has dedicated her life to land-based healing and learning.[65]

Morrison's work has been central to the Northwest Coast Indigenous food sovereignty movement, and she was one of the first people to utilize the concept of food sovereignty in creating spaces for dialogue and action. In August 2006 she coordinated the first annual Interior of B.C. Indigenous Food Sovereignty Conference. The conference focused on the development of regional networks and community-based, culturally relevant action plans that promote the protection, conservation, and restoration of Indigenous food systems and that work to ensure that traditional Indigenous hunters, fishermen, and gatherers in the interior of British Columbia have access to their traditional foodways.[66] For the last thirteen years, Morrison has led community-based, regional, and international decolonizing food systems discourse, creating a critical pathway where Indigenous food sovereignty meets social justice, climate change, and food systems research, action, and adaptive policy, planning, and governance.[67] Morrison also manages the Wild Salmon Caravan Team created in 2014, the purpose of which is to "build capacity of coalitions and campaigns that link Indigenous and non-Indigenous peoples, artists, food systems networks, individuals, organizations, and communities who are working to protect, conserve and restore wild salmon and its habitat in the Fraser Basin and Salish Seas corridor."[68] In 2019 Morrison and the WGIFS launched the Indigenous Food and Freedom School to support food sovereignty initiatives in British Columbia through restoration and regeneration of sustainable Indigenous food systems.[69]

Indigenous peoples are revitalizing their traditional food systems, practices, and knowledge by utilizing their own food principles and philosophies, which has framed Indigenous scholarship such as Mariaelena Huambachano's research on the "good living philosophies" of the Andean people of Peru and the Māori of Aotearoa, New Zealand, and Michelle Daigle's work on the Anishinaabe law of mino bimaadiziwin, "living the good life."[70] Huambachano (Quechua) defines good living philosophies as the "collective, harmonious, and spiritual approach to the preservation of all life forms," which is at the center of Quechua and Māori food security.[71] These philosophies, Huambachano asserts, are grounded in cultural and environmental principles that pervade and infuse holistic practices "that preserve and cultivate the ecological and social conditions necessary for the continuance of their intrinsic connection with the land."[72] Quechua and Māori intergenerational accumulation of ancestral knowledge is centered in what Huambachano describes as an "Indigenous cosmovision," creating a harmonious and holistic relationship between humans, nonhumans, and nonliving things, which is the basis for food security and sovereignty.[73] She connects Quechua and Māori food sovereignty to their self-determination, struggles for autonomy, and "regaining control over their overall wellbeing."[74]

Daigle (Mushkegowuk/Swampy Cree) focuses her research on the Anishinaabe people in Ontario, Canada, and their efforts to protect and renew harvesting grounds and waters that sustain their traditional foodways, which are rooted in their law of mino bimaadiziwin and the principle of "living the good life."[75] She quotes Anishinaabe elder Ogiimaagwanebiik, who bases mino bimaadiziwin in reciprocity and relationships: "It is about helping one another and respecting the Creator's creation, mutual respect. It is about sharing [our traditional foods]. I think it is also about being thankful."[76] To illuminate the law of mino bimaadiziwin, Daigle uses as an example the revitalization of the Anishinaabe fall harvest, where in precolonial gatherings, communities across Anishinaabe territory would prepare, process, trade, and gift foods. These harvests strengthened political and economic relationships through the protocols and ceremonies attached to this event.[77] Today the reviving of the harvest also rebuilds and reinforces relationships between youth, adults, and elders, where Anishinaabe foods and ecological knowledge are transferred as youth are mentored and taught food processing and preparation.[78] Like Haumbachano, Daigle connects the revitalization of Anishinaabe foodways and "living and acting on relational responsibilities and accountabilities" to their struggles for autonomy and self-determination; efforts that are not constrained by "the oppressive parameters of settler colonial authorities and jurisdictions."[79]

tiičʕaqƛ: Nuu-chah-nulth Food Sovereignty

My people, the Nuu-chah-nulth, are restoring respectful and meaningful relationships with our environment that are situated within the concept of food sovereignty. We are actively engaging decolonization and sustainable self-determination through reinstatement of authority over our ḥaḥuułi, ancestral territory, and through the development of strategies and implementation of policies aimed at the sustainable production and consumption of traditional foods through ecologically sound food systems. Our Nuu-chah-nulth communities maintain the understanding that we must honor the wisdom and values of ancestral knowledge in maintaining responsible and respectful relationships with the natural world; therefore, these efforts are grounded in Nuu-chah-nulth philosophies of hišukʔiš ćawaak,[80] everything is interconnected; ʔuʔaałuk, to take care of; and ʔiisaak, to be respectful, as discussed in the introduction to this book.

In March 2005 the Nuu-chah-nulth Tribal Council (NTC), which provides services and support to fourteen Nuu-chah-nulth Nations, launched Uu-a-thluk, an aquatic resource management organization administered through the NTC. The vision of Uu-a-thluk is to "take care of" the ḥaḥuułi in a way that is consistent with Nuu-chah-nulth values and principles, a responsibility given to our people through ńaas, our Creator.[81] The organization is guided by a Council of Ḥawiiḥ (hereditary chiefs) who meet three times a year to provide guidance and direction through the sharing of ecological knowledge and ancestral wisdom with the staff and seasonal interns. This philosophy of marine management is consistent with efforts to become sustainable, self-determining nations and reinforces the ruling authority of our ḥawiłp̓atak ḥawiiḥ, traditional governance.[82]

One of the main functions of Uu-a-thluk is to manage and protect our marine foods and the habitats in which they thrive, and to work with non-Indigenous governmental authorities in creating management schemes that are culturally sensitive and include Nuu-chah-nulth ecological knowledge. Our communities depend on salmon for our cultural and economic survival and for our tiičʕaqƛ, holistic health. Uu-a-thluk works at protecting and advancing Nuu-chah-nulth salmon fishing rights through the T'aaq-wiihak Fishery, meaning "fishing with permission of the ḥaẇiiḥ," and provides training, education, mentorship, and workplace opportunities to get more community members involved in salmon and marine management.[83] Uu-a-thluk is framed within the overarching Nuu-chah-nulth philosophy of hišukʔiš čawaak, that protecting our marine foods and ecosystems for ceremonial and societal sustenance needs is at the center of our food sovereignty efforts and vital to restoring tiičʕaqƛ in our communities.

While these food sovereignty initiatives continue to expand and flourish, Indigenous people continue to face challenges to enacting food sovereignty. This is exemplified in the antiwhaling protest that arose when the Makah Tribe in Washington State announced in 1994 that it was reviving its tradition of hunting whales, a conflict I analyze in my 2010 book *Spirits of Our Whaling Ancestors: Revitalizing Makah and Nuu-chah-nulth Traditions*.

Settler Colonialism, Culinary Imperialism, and Contemporary Challenges to Enacting Food Sovereignty: The 1999 Makah Whale Hunt

In 1999 the Makah tribe on the western tip of Washington State harvested a sixʷaˑwix̌,[84] the Makah word for gray whale, and with one throw of their harpoon they enacted food sovereignty by revitalizing and reinforcing a cultural tradition that is central to their identities. For the qʷidiččaʔaˑtx̌[85] or Makah, and my people, the Nuu-chah-nulth, whaling was the foundation of our political, social, spiritual, and economic structures. However, colonization, federal policies, and the depletion of whales as a result of an unregulated West Coast whaling industry, forced us to put away our harpoons in the early 1900s.[86] Before the arrival of mamałńi, white settlers, the Indigenous people in the Northwest Coast lived in natural environments that were rich in material goods and a variety of foods. Our marine-based economies provided us with a wealth of foods that not only sustained our communities but were nutritious, rich in vitamins and minerals. Our societies maintained optimum health by consuming large quantities of meat, fat, and oil from whales and

1.1 Cutting up the gray whale—the Makah Tribe's 1999 whale hunt. *Photograph courtesy of Debbie Ross-Preston, Northwest Indian Fisheries Commission.*

other sea mammals that provided us with health-promoting nourishment and an overall sense of well-being.[87] Studies conducted among the Indigenous people in northern Canada and Alaska affirm the health benefits of eating whale, finding that a diet rich in sea mammal oil dramatically decreased the risk of death from heart disease, reduced symptoms of diabetes, and helped alleviate symptoms of arthritis and other chronic diseases.[88]

Three significant factors were key in the Makah tribe's decision to revive their whale hunts. First, the gray whale, the main whale the Makah hunted, rebounded from near extinction to the point where they could be sustainably hunted again, and in 1994 the species was removed from the Endangered Species List. Second, in the 1970s a major storm uncovered thousands of whaling artifacts in the abandoned Makah village of Ozette, sparking a cultural renaissance among tribal members and a renewed interest in their whaling tradition. Third, in the 1974 case *United States v. Washington* (also known as the Boldt decision), Judge Boldt reaffirmed the Washington state tribe's treaty rights, with one of these rights exclusive to the Makah tribe being the right to hunt whales. These factors created an opportunity for the Makah tribe to restore their whale hunts, placing them within a larger context of cultural revitalization and self-determination movements that Indigenous peoples were experiencing since the 1960s.[89] The Nuu-chah-nulth, following the lead of our Makah relatives, announced the decision to revitalize our whale hunts as well, understanding this as a necessary process of decolonization and a strategy for enriching and strengthening our cultures and reaffirming our identities as whaling people.[90]

While the Makah tribe's whale hunt was received with overwhelming support from people and nations throughout the world, there were also those who opposed it and began organizing an antiwhaling campaign immediately after the Makah's announcement in 1994. The antiwhaling coalition consisted of a wide range of interests, from environmental groups to right-wing politicians, who effectively waged a campaign in the court of public opinion that relied on false stereotypes and misconceived ideas to discredit the Makah and Nuu-chah-nulth people's whaling cultures. In response to a Canadian radio program on the Makah tribe reviving their tradition of hunting whales, a reader wrote:

> Personally, I think it is a stupid, senseless, and needless slaughter by a bunch of jerks. They didn't go out in their canoes as their forefathers had done, with spears, etc., no they went out with a motor driven craft, armed with high caliber rifles and took unfair advantage of a creature that was not bothering them. . . . Who do they think they are? . . . They still appear to be ruthless savages.[91]

In a letter to the *Seattle Times* a reader responded to this notion of revitalizing tradition, writing:

I am anxious to know where I may apply for a license to kill Indians. My forefathers helped settle the west and it was their tradition to kill every Redskin they saw. "The only good Indian is a dead Indian," they believed. I also want to keep faith with my ancestors.[92]

When the Makah tribe began preparing for their hunt, members of the anti-whaling coalition condemned it, arguing that the hunt was not "traditional" because the Makah were using motorized boats, high-powered weapons, and cellular phones, ultimately denying us the very right that all societies strive toward—the right to cultural change and technological advancement.[93] Makah tribal member Janine Bowechop, director of the Makah Cultural and Research Center, responded to this argument:

> For some reason some people like to freeze us in the past. If you're not doing something the way it was done prior to contact, then you're not doing it right—you're not doing it in the Native way. But we allow other cultures to make changes. One of my friends said, "I'm a White American but I don't make my butter in a butter churn anymore, and I'm not criticized for that." . . . Folks don't ride around in covered wagons anymore, but we don't turn around and say, "Gee, you're not a real American. . . . But, unfortunately, we're continually criticized if we do anything different than we did 500 years ago.[94]

One of the main arguments against the Makah tribe was centered in a foods-based discourse with members of the coalition arguing that the Makah and Nuu-chah-nulth peoples did not need to hunt whales for food because we had all the food we needed.[95] Indigenous peoples globally have struggled to control access to and production of their food sources as the colonizing nations appropriated our lands, and through a history of Western hegemonic control over food production and consumption that kept us from our traditional food sources.[96] Through these assertions of cultural and culinary imperialism, people from other cultures continue to impose their own symbolic and aesthetic food values on our societies, making it difficult for Indigenous peoples to reconnect to their traditional foods. And through their political power, wealthy Western states and NGOs influence what is acceptable as food and what animals or mammals should or should not be eaten. The antiwhaling discourse that arose over killing and eating whales was couched in moral and legal terms, but as ecologist Russel Barsh maintains, the larger issue is one of power—the power to determine what we eat.

> Privileged societies have acquired the power to determine what the world eats and to impose their own symbolic and aesthetic food taboos on others. Placed in proper historical context, contemporary efforts to abolish whaling and sealing are exposed as the flip side of Western European domination of world food supplies. . . . Moral indignation, rather than conservation, has driven the antiharvesting campaigns for the last twenty-five years.[97]

In my culture we have an understanding that we all exist, humans, animals, plants, etc., in a shared environment where we are all equal. Indigenous cultures thrive in a world of reciprocity between us and our environment. Our relationship with animals has always been one based on respect and gratitude and there is a sense of sacredness attached to the spirit of the animal for giving itself to us for sustenance. The First Species Ceremonies of my people, for example, is a sacred event that affirms the "personhood" of these animals and mammals and honors them for giving themselves to feed us. And within this symbiotic relationship is the understanding that death is ultimately integrated into life. The whaling opponents saw the death of the whale through a Western cultural lens and, thus, ignored the spiritual and sacred elements attached to the Makah and Nuu-chah-nulth whaling tradition.[98]

Indigenous peoples have always been respectful custodians and protectors of the environments that provided them and their future generations with sustenance. The land, water, and the plants, animals, and their habitats were safeguarded to maintain their sustainability.[99] In an Indigenous worldview, plants and animals that provide us with food are seen as "spiritual gifts,"[100] and their spirits are honored through rituals and prayers that are passed down through ancestral knowledge to the following generations.[101] In the Northwest Coast, we have many First Foods ceremonies honoring the spirits of the animals and plants that give their lives to feed us. For example, as discussed in the next chapter, our coastal marine space provides an exceptionally rich and nurturing environment for salmon and a sustainable balance between salmon and human ecosystems evolved through thousands of years, developing into a respectful and reciprocal relationship.

I have written about our Nuu-chah-nulth whaling tradition and how special rituals, prayers, taboos, and ceremonies were central to a successful whale
hunt, which was attributed to the ḥaẃiɫ, chief, and his ḥakum, wife, and which
developed a respectful and sacred relationship with the animal. If they and
the whaling crew adhered to the proper protocols and ritual preparations, they
then earned respect from the whale's spirit, and the whale allowed itself to
be taken as food for them and their community.[102] This is exemplified in the
Nuu-chah-nulth story of the great Ahousaht whaler Keesta, as told by Umeek,
Richard Atleo, in his book, *Tsawalk: A Nuu-chah-nulth Worldview*. Keesta, Umeek's
great-grandfather, was born in 1866 and was raised to be a whaling ḥaẃiɫ.
Throughout his lifetime he would ʔuusimč, which is a rigorous spiritual cleansing
that involved prayer, fasting, and observances of taboos.[103] Keesta understood
that a successful hunt meant creating this sacred relationship and that "the great
personage of the whale demanded the honor of extended ceremony."[104]

> Every protocol had been observed between the whaling chief and the
> spirit of the whale. Keesta . . . had thrown the harpoon, and the whale
> had accepted it, had grabbed and held onto the harpoon according
> to the agreement they had made through prayers and petitions. Har-
> mony prevailed, whale and whaler were one.

Animals and plants that gave themselves to us as food nourished not only
our bodies but also our souls. The rituals practiced around our haʔum created
what Indigenous scholar Clara Sue Kidwell (White Earth Chippewa/Choctaw)
describes as a "sense of communion."[105] Animals and plants are considered
our relatives, a concept that many non-Indigenous peoples have difficulty in
understanding because they do not have—or have lost—their own spiritual
relationship to the foods they eat. The physical act of eating plants and animals,
Kidwell says, reinforces the social and sacred bonds we have to their spirits that
give themselves as food.

> Consuming food is the most basic form of establishing relationships
> among humans, plants, animals, and the forces in the environment
> that are the ultimate sources of life. It is an integral element of both
> physical and spiritual being. Gifts of food solidify human relation-

ships; offerings of plant and animal life establish and maintain relationships between humans and the spiritual world.[106]

Viewed from this standpoint of animals and plants as gifts, a culture of gratitude is embedded within the relationship between humans and nonhumans,
where reciprocity is the foundation. Animals and plants that are treated with
respect will, in turn, provide their physical forms as food and are regarded as
"gifts from the earth," says Robin Kimmerer, which establishes a particular
relationship, an obligation of sorts to give, to receive, and to reciprocate.[107]

Indigenous food traditions are central to food sovereignty and security and
they reinforce familial and social bonds of generosity and reciprocity in harvesting, sharing, and eating our haʔum, or traditional foods. For the Makah,
the capture, distribution, sharing, and eating of the sixʷaʔwix̌ they harvested in
1999 strengthened their community; revived prayers, songs, ceremonies, and
stories integral to their whaling tradition; and strengthened their cultural identity as whalers. Enacting food sovereignty through the revival of their whaling
practices reaffirmed the spiritual, emotional, and physical relationships the
Makah have to their waterways and to the whale. After the hunt they followed
the tradition passed down from their whaling ancestors. After all the sacred
rituals were conducted to show respect to the whale's spirit and to the whale
for giving itself to the Makah people, tribal members held a huge Potlatch in
honor of this historic event to thank the people who supported the revival of
their hunts. On May 22, 1999, more than three thousand people came to the
small Makah village of Neah Bay to share in the celebration and to show their
support for the revitalization of the Makah tribe's whaling tradition. There were
people from the local Native and non-Native communities, people from tribes
across the United States and from the First Nations communities in Canada, and
people from throughout the world, as far away as Africa.

The Makah people sang songs and performed dances for their guests and
to honor the return of the whale to their community. Living up to their Makah
name, meaning "generous with food," the tribal members provided their guests
with a traditional feast, serving them heaping plates filled with salmon, halibut,
steamed clams, and oysters. And for the first time in over eighty years, whale
was the main food on the menu. The Makah were excited about offering such
an important food to their guests, and they experimented with various ways

to prepare it so that even those with more finicky palates would enjoy it. The whale meat was baked, roasted, and broiled. The blubber was served both cooked and raw. Many people from our Nuu-chah-nulth communities attended the celebration and partook in the tasting of our shared traditional food for the very first time. Nuu-chah-nulth member Denise Ambrose said sharing in this feast of whale meat made her feel proud to be Nuu-chah-nulth.

> This was the first time that I would taste whale meat, a food that I, as a Nuu-chah-nulth person, should have been brought up on. The meat looked somewhat like dark chicken meat. To me, it smelled and tasted like corned beef. It is hard to describe my feelings after tasting the roasted meat. I was proud to be Nuu-chah-nulth-aht. . . . So many other [Nuu-chah-nulth] people have passed on without having the opportunity to share in what was the most integral part of our culture: the whale. I felt honoured.[108]

Two years after the Makah whale hunt, the Makah Cultural and Research Center administered a survey of the Makah households to clarify and quantify the reactions of Makah tribal members to the revival of their whaling practices. The results of the Makah Household Whaling Survey were overwhelmingly positive, with over 95 percent of the respondents indicating full support for restoring their whale hunts. The survey also indicated an eagerness of all Makah members to incorporate more traditions and cultural practices into their daily lives.[109] A second Makah Household Whaling Survey was conducted in 2006 to see if the Makah people still supported continuing their whale hunts. The responses were still overwhelmingly positive for whaling. Over 88 percent of the Makah people surveyed believed that revitalizing their whaling tradition was a positive move, especially for its cultural value and political importance, and continued their support of their whale hunts.[110]

Food sovereignty is the right to healthy and culturally appropriate food defined through our own cultural food practices, but in December 2002 a Ninth Circuit Court of Appeals decision legally stopped the Makah tribe from exercising this right, and their cultural and treaty right, by banning their whale hunts. In *Anderson v. Evans* (314 F.3d 1006), the court ruled that Makah whaling must cease until the tribe prepares an environmental impact statement (EIS) under the National Environmental Policy Act (NEPA), which is more stringent than the

Environmental Assessment (EA) that was conducted for the 1999 hunt.[111] The court also determined that the Marine Mammal Protection Act (MMPA) applied to the Makah tribe and that their 1855 treaty, which affirmed and protected their whaling right, did not exempt them from the scrutiny of this act.[112] The Makah were now required to obtain an MMPA waiver from the federal government through the National Oceanic and Atmospheric Administration (NOAA), which could authorize a whaling quota.[113]

In examining the Makah tribe's efforts to revitalize their whaling tradition, we see the complexities and challenges that Indigenous peoples face when attempting to enact food sovereignty. Indigenous scholars such as Kyle Powys Whyte (Potawatomi) place these challenges squarely within colonialism and as a derivative of settler colonial domination and food injustice. Food injustice, Whyte maintains, is a violation of Indigenous collective self-determination over their food systems:

> Food injustice can manifest as violations of food sovereignty that some Indigenous people associate with the destruction of particular foods or food systems. Violations of food sovereignty are one strategy of colonial societies, such as U.S. settler colonialism, to undermine Indigenous collective continuance in Indigenous peoples' own homelands.[114]

It has been more than twenty years since the Makah threw the harpoon that reaffirmed their cultural identity as whaling people, and since then their cultural and treaty right to whaling has been tied up in political and legal challenges fueled by racial and food injustice that are at the core of settler colonialism. The destruction of Indigenous foodways was one of the many colonial erasures utilized by settler society in their attempts to dismantle Indigenous lifeways, and its weakening of our political, economic, social, and spiritual systems continues to this day. The ban on the Potlatch, the refusal to allow Indigenous children to speak their languages or practice their spirituality in boarding schools, the removal from ancestral homelands, the attempt to replace our ḥaw̓iiḥ, hereditary chief system, with an elected governing system—these are some of the many ways in which colonial erasure was used against us, along with removing us from our traditional foods. Violating Indigenous food sovereignty, Whyte asserts, "is a strategy of settler colonial domination that erases Indigenous capacities for exercising collective self-determination."[115]

ċuumaʕas

The River That Runs through Us,
the Communal Fish Pot

A happy Tseshaht has a drum in one hand and a sockeye in the other.
—DARRELL ROSS SR.

Y OU ENTER my community of Tseshaht by driving across a bridge called the Orange Bridge (although it was painted silver many years ago, we still refer to it by this name), which clearly demarcates our community from the city of Port Alberni.[1] The bridge crosses a river we call ċuumaʕas, meaning "cleansing or washing,"[2] but that became known as the Somass River, a name used by the mamałni (white settlers) who began moving into our territory in the mid-1800s. The river begins at the mouth of the Alberni Inlet, forty kilometers in length, which flows into Barkley Sound and out into the Pacific Ocean. The Somass River joins with two other rivers, Stamp and Sproat, which drain from Sproat Lake and Great Central Lake. I grew up on the Somass River, which flows a few hundred yards behind my family home.

My fondest childhood memories are of spending endless hours with my relatives swimming, boating, and fishing on this river. We were raised to understand the importance of this river but to also understand its dangers. When I was a baby, to make me familiar with the water, my mother would walk out into it and hold me in the water, where I would flap my arms and kick my legs uncontrollably. Eventually, after much flapping and kicking, I figured out how to use them to swim. Thanks to my mother's training and preparation, I became a master swimmer and learned how to navigate the strong tides and swift currents at a very young age.

When I was young, the miʕaat, our word for sockeye salmon, were so plentiful that there were shallow places in the river where you could walk and you would feel the salmon swimming between your legs. Having this plentiful salmon supply made us dependent on it as an abundant and healthy food source, and many people in my community became avid fishers, including myself. Behind my grandparents' home next door to where I grew up, there were large fields with abandoned farming equipment, markers, and other fragments of colonization from the Canadian government's attempt to make us into farmers. As if we would give up our salmon and cultural connections to water for what—potatoes? My great-grandfather Watty Watts had sown these fields, but after he passed away no one kept them up. Still, my family and community members continued to pick the apples, plums, and pears that grew in the fruit orchard created by the Indian agents. As an ironic turn to colonialism, the land that the agents cleared for us to farm became an ideal place where many of my male relatives and community members carved cedar čapac (canoes) that were used for fishing for salmon in the river.

On warm sunny afternoons my cousins and I would head to the back fields to watch the men as they carved their čapac, which were typically around eight to ten feet long. We would position ourselves on the slight hill under a large chestnut tree overlooking the field where they all contentedly worked. Some days we would take our lunches with us, usually salmon sandwiches and fruit plucked from one of the trees in the orchard, and as we ate we would listen to the men tell stories, crack jokes, catch up on community gossip, and share their knowledge of canoe carving with each other and with us. When their stories, jokes, or gossip got too mature for our young ears, they would switch over to speaking in our language. We would listen intently, trying to figure out what they were saying. I learned some of my best "bad" words in my language from those canoe-carving afternoons. Rain or shine, those men would be out there, sculpting, steaming, and carving their čapac until they were ready to go. When the canoe got its final touches, they would all put down their carving tools and get ready to help the owner carry it to the small sandy beach that was a few hundred yards away. Sometimes, if there were not enough men there to carry the čapac , we were asked to help out, which we gladly did. We would turn the canoe over and each of us would grab the edge and lift it up and then gently carry it down to the beach. The čapac was ready to meet ćuumaʕas. Many people in my community carved and used these wooden canoes right up to the 1970s, when they began being replaced by aluminum canoes and boats. The canoes were kept at this small beach behind my grandparents' home, and the owners allowed us to use them as long as we took care of them and brought them back to the beach in one piece.

Because my cousins and I spent endless hours on the river in these canoes, we became master paddlers at a very young age. When the canoes were not being used by their owners we would take them out on the river for an afternoon of fishing or we would just paddle contently down the Somass River in the slow-moving current, stopping every now and then to take a dive in the cool water; sometimes we would pull up along the riverbank to do some exploring. Our favorite place to fish was McCoy Creek, which is a small waterway that connects to the river and snakes around my family home. It becomes quite shallow in the summer, which made it much easier to catch small salmon and trout there. We would bait our hooks with worms and drop our fishing lines into the water, praying that we would catch a nice fish. Usually we ended up catching a nasty bullhead, not a fish you would want to eat, and we would throw it back in the water. It was sheer joy when we finally caught some salmon or a couple of trout! We would put our fish in a bucket and paddle back to the beach and then run up to my grandparents' home to show them, our faces beaming with pride. If my grandpa was not too busy, he would offer to cook them, and we would all sit at the table squirming impatiently as he boiled, baked, or pan-fried them. Once they were cooked, Grandpa would place our "prize" catches in front of us, and we would dig in. As we feasted, my grandpa would watch us, a little grin on his face as his grandchildren upheld their connection to ćuumaʕas and to the fish from its water that provided us with nutritional and cultural sustenance.

The Centrality of Salmon to Coastal Indigenous
Peoples and Cultures

The Somass River streams through our territory like a vein of life, bringing the precious salmon that nourish and feed our community. Salmon is at the heart of our stories and shared experiences; it is the foundation of our culture and has remained an important nutritional food in our diets. In this chapter I share stories from my community to elucidate the centrality of salmon to Tseshaht food sovereignty and to our nutritional, physical, and spiritual health. Through harvesting, processing, and sharing salmon, we Tseshaht continue to reinforce our cultural bonds to one another, to our salmon relatives, and to ċuumaʕas. I show how maintaining a connection to this traditional and nutritional food connects us, figuratively, literally, and culturally to our ancestral homelands.

The Tseshaht were created on a small island that makes up what is now called the Broken Group Islands. We started off as a small group and through amalgamations with other groups we grew and expanded our territory through the islands, Barkley Sound, up through the Alberni Inlet, and into the lower Somass River.[3] Tseshaht practiced a seasonal round of food as we traveled throughout our ancestral marine spaces, harvesting foods and staying at various village sites along the way. We made our way from one resource harvesting area to another, collecting and harvesting the sea mammals, fish, and other seafood as well as terrestrial animals, plants, roots, or berries at each site. By the late fall the fishers, harvesters, and gatherers would reconvene at our winter village site along the Somass River, where they would partake in winter ceremonies and Potlatches. However, colonization forced us onto reserve lands and limited or removed our access to our summer villages, where we harvested and collected food. By the mid-1800s we began living year-round in the village of saaʔaḥi on the Somass River, which is where our community is located today.[4]

The Northwest Coast provides an exceptionally rich and nurturing environment for salmon as well as a sustainable balance between salmon and human ecosystems, which has evolved through thousands of years into a respectful and reciprocal relationship. Of course, other animal species were significant in the maintenance of this balanced ecosystem. For example, salmon is a main food staple for black and brown bears living in the Northwest Coast. The bears drag salmon into the forests and the parts that are uneaten will decompose, leaving nitrogen and other marine nutrients that are important to plant and tree growth.

These nutrients are also spread through the bear's urine and feces.[5] Other creatures such as birds, insects, and crabs eat and transfer nutrients, which, as environmental studies professor Kyle Powys Whyte (Potawatomi) explains in ecological terms, demonstrates how salmon plays a major role in contributing "to healthy forest ecosystems."[6]

Salmon was a primary food source that allowed coastal cultures to flourish, and this was never taken for granted. The spirit of the salmon was celebrated through the First Salmon Ceremony that honored its return each year and maintained this important relationship. In the coastal Indigenous belief system, everything has a spirit.[7] The salmon's spirit is intimately tied to our societies and is shown the greatest respect and honor. During the first salmon run, tribal members gather along the waterways to catch the first salmon. These salmon are ceremonially cut up and divided among the guests to eat. While eating the salmon, prayers and ceremonies are conducted to show respect to their spirits and to thank them for bringing their physical bodies to our communities to feed us. Once all the ceremonies have been conducted and all the fish have been eaten, the remaining bones and skin are collected and returned to the water. The spirits of the salmon return to their homes in the deep ocean waters, where they share with their relatives the great respect that was shown to them. This ensures that our salmon relatives continue to visit us and provide their physical forms to us as food.[8]

In his fieldwork with the Nuu-chah-nulth-aht,[9] anthropologist Philip Drucker noted the importance of strict observances of these rituals, such as making sure all of the salmon bones were returned to the river. He recounts a prayer conducted by a ḥaw̓ił (chief) to the spirits of the salmon, indicating that they would be treated with respect and honor for bringing this nutritious food to our communities each year.

> The [chief] sprinkled them with [eagle] down and "talked" to them saying, "We are glad you have come to visit us; we have been saving these (feathers) for you for a long time. We have been waiting a long time for you, and hope you will visit us soon."[10]

With access to many fishing areas in the Somass River, Alberni Inlet, and around the Broken Group Islands, the Tseshaht harvested a variety of salmon utilizing different methods to catch and process them. This iconic species of the

Northwest Coast plays a critical role in supporting and maintaining the region's ecological health, and it is entwined in the social fabric of our Indigenous cultures and food traditions. Indigenous peoples have a cultural concept of "food as medicine," which promotes a holistic approach to maintaining and restoring the dietary, emotional, and spiritual health of our bodies. It means maintaining the ecosystems that provide us with food.[11] Wild salmon is high in protein, low in saturated fat, and rich in omega-3 fatty acids. Numerous studies have shown how essential fatty acids derived from fish and sea mammal oils reduce the risks of heart disease and type 2 diabetes.[12] Omega-3 fatty acids can also reduce inflammation that can cause heart disease, stroke, autoimmune disorders, and certain types of cancer.[13] Omega-3 fatty acids, along with Omega-6 fatty acids, are classified as polyunsaturated fats, and research has found that their consumption supports both our physical and mental health and reduces the risk of depression, dementia, psychosis, and ADHD.[14]

Ask any person from a Northwest Coast tribal community about the foods they grew up with, and the first one they most often mention is salmon. It was and still is integral to our spiritual and cultural identity and plays a major role in our nutritional health as well as the health of our ecosystems, with the nutrients they carry through our waterways and the animals that depend on them for food. Therefore, maintaining our cultural and spiritual ties to salmon and protecting its habitats are crucial to our very survival as people, putting this at the heart of our food sovereignty.

The Northwest Coast is home to some of the most diverse and richest Indigenous cultures in the world, nations that flourished in abundances of marine mammals and dense vegetation in an area with mild winters and moist summers.[15] Before colonization forced political, social, spiritual, and economic societal change, our cultures and economies were marine-based, where we derived most of our sustenance from the oceans, inlets, and rivers that flow through our territories. These waterways provided an abundance of food and, intertwined with the rainforest, provided the basis for an impressive material culture. Our rich marine and coastal environment supported the development of societies with large populations and permanent residences, and permitted the development of complex social hierarchies with permanent leadership positions reinforced through the Potlatch system.[16]

The Potlatch tradition was, and still is, at the center of our coastal societies. At its most basic understanding, the Potlatch was a public event hosted by ḥaẃiiḥ (chiefs) to validate and reinforce status, wealth, and hereditary privileges acquired at birth, especially rights and stewardship over territories recognized as part of their ḥaḥuułi (ancestral homelands).[17] The Potlatch had political, economic, social, and spiritual aspects that served to reinforce our cultures, languages, and societies, which is why colonial and federal officials tried to eradicate these ceremonies as part of their attempt to control us and assimilate us into the Canadian and US social order. Between 1884 and 1951 Canada enforced a law making it a crime for coastal peoples to hold or participate in a Potlatch. Nonetheless, our Potlatches persevered and remain embedded within our cultures.

The word Potlatch comes from the Chinook trade language and was derived from one of our Nuu-chah-nulth words, p̓ačiƛ, which means "to give." Potlatches reinforce reciprocity, uphold social obligations, strengthen familial ties, and reaffirm respectful relationships between human and nonhuman kinfolk. Food was, and still is, at the core of the Potlatch, and the sharing of food was entwined in the cultural, political, and social elements that framed this tradition, as explained by Tseshaht elder, author, and cultural leader George Clutesi in his 1969 book, *Potlatch*.

> The food came steaming out of the large containers and from the ever-expectant guests there was an audible, Hhooooooooo! Chooooooo! Choo, choo, choo, choc ho! An expression common to all people of the coast for a complete and agreeable surprise. The food offered by the ruler of the tribe was winter spring salmon, the Soo-hah. Broth in the feast-dishes was kept and served in wooden basins into which whole families dipped gleaming white clamshells to sip the rich taste of the Soo-hah. Other men served sockeye, cohoe and summer spring salmon which had all been smoked and well-dried in the summer and in the fall. . . . Liberal quantities of the oil was provided and the guests partook of the oils liberally. . . . And all the people of the confederacy shared alike according to their appetite—thus demonstrating again, without words, the whole purpose of the laws and customs of the coast.[18]

My family has held many Potlatches over the years, and these are times that bring us all together in the harvesting and processing of the foods that will be shared with our guests as part of the feasting that takes place. A few years ago my family was getting ready to host a Potlatch and made plans to host a luncheon for community members. About a week after sending out invitations for the Potlatch later that year, I was visiting my Aunty Misbun in the late afternoon and someone knocked on her door. My aunt opened the door and there on her doorstep was a hind quarter of a deer. At the bottom of the step was one of our community members, who said, "I heard your family is planning a feast so I wanted to help out. čuu."[19] And there we were, holding our afternoon beverages, staring down at half a deer that was still warm. My aunt made a few phone calls, got hold of some relatives with sharp knives, and the deer was cut up, put into bags, and stored in the freezer. At our Potlatch a few months later, the deer was made into a savory stew that we shared with all our guests.

Because the environment was so rich with diversity, our societies were able to focus on certain foods and animals and plants that provided the greatest return, like salmon. Salmon played a major role in the development of large village populations along the coast because it preserves and stores well. As discussed in chapter 1, through their birthright our ḥaẁiiḥ, chiefs, had claims to exclusive ownership to certain ḥaḥuułi, ancestral homelands, which extended to the animals, fish, seafood, and plants that they controlled and managed as stewards for their ʔuuštaqimł, their family or lineage group, and the masčim, community members. The ʔuuštaqimł and masčim contributed their labor to the upkeep of the salmon, with the ḥaẁił (chief) rewarding their labor by receiving a share of this food. Nuu-chah-nulth elder Roy Haiyupis articulates the meaning of ḥaḥuułi as more than just a sense of territorial ownership and that it is embedded in the chief's responsibilities to the lands, waters, and plants and to his ʔuuštaqimł and masčim.[20]

Traditional salmon stock management was built on sustainability with cultural sanctions in place, and transfer of ecological and ancestral knowledge of salmon life cycles, to ensure their continual return. Coastal Indigenous peoples understood the cyclical and predictable nature of these salmon runs, and we had complex technological, social, and ritual practices in place to harvest the fish, which were the basis of our subsistence economies.[21] Settler society failed to acknowledge or understand this sophisticated ecological knowledge, believing instead that coastal Indigenous peoples had no cultural understanding of salmon spawning cycles or habitat protection methods. For example, anthropologist Philip Drucker, who conducted fieldwork among the Nuu-chah-nulth communities in the 1930s, writes, "It is doubtful whether the Indians understood the life cycle of these fish, . . . or connected the spawning with the tiny new-hatched par, or these with the adult salmon."[22] But Coastal Indigenous oral history and ethnographic information prove otherwise, dispelling this ignorance. There is ample evidence that Indigenous societies sustained and enhanced salmon populations by transplanting salmon eggs to other waterways and creating spawning populations in areas where there was no prior spawning population, or by bolstering declining fish stocks.[23] The Tlingit are known to have removed beaver dams on rivers that blocked sockeye salmon spawning areas upriver and rearranging rocks to improve water flow to increase and support salmon spawning habitat. Extensive oral and ethnographic data show how Indigenous people including the Nuu-chah-nulth-aht manipulated their environments through practices such as field burning to increase productivity.[24]

Indigenous ecological knowledge demonstrated a well- developed and complex understanding of the environment. Tseshaht, like other coastal Indigenous Nations, have within their worldview the understanding of thirteen moons in a calendar year that represented cyclical changes, and moons were named for the seasonal harvesting, hunting, fishing, and gathering activities that occurred during this time period. For example, the huyaaqimł, the wild geese or flying geese moon, in May denotes the beginning of whaling season, when the geese arrive. The qawašimł or berry moon in June tells us that it is time to harvest certain berries. Many of our moons directly link to salmon harvesting periods and would determine the species of fish that would be available during this time period—for example, the saċupimł, the spring or king salmon moon, in August; the hinkuuʔasimł or dog salmon moon in September: and the čiyaaqimł or cutting fish moon in October.[25] I remember my Grandpa Hughie looking at the moon when I was a young girl and telling me that it would be time to harvest the berries soon or that the miʕaat (sockeye salmon) would soon be coming to the Somass River. I would look at the moon trying to figure out what my grandpa saw that I did not see. I did not realize at the time that he was raised with this cultural understanding of lunar phases.

Northwest Coast Indigenous peoples harvest five species of Pacific salmon: sockeye, chinook, coho, chum, and pink, with all of them sharing the same biological characteristics. They are all anadromous, born in freshwater lakes, rivers, and streams, then they eventually make their way to the open sea, where they spend most of their lives. At ages of one to five years, depending on the species, the fish move in cohorts or runs, making their way back to the fresh waters where they were born so that they can spawn and die.[26] Salmon harvesting technology was well developed and included items such as spears, drift or dip nets, and fish weirs. We Tseshaht developed the yaḥaak or fish weir, which was the most sophisticated and economically rewarding, allowing large quantities of salmon to be harvested at a time when runs were at their peak.[27]

The ḥaẁiiḥ controlled the yaḥaak and demonstrated a keen sense of conservation knowledge and skill by determining harvesting periods and the types of fish that would be harvested. The yaḥaak were erected along the rivers to catch salmon as they were making their way to their spawning grounds. They were made from long pieces of wood and held together to make an underwater fence that was strategically placed in areas where the salmon followed the currents upstream. During low tides, the fish would get caught in these weirs where they could then be easily removed. During high tide, the fish could swim over the weirs and make their way upstream to their spawning grounds. The yaḥaak would be opened to allow an adequate amount to pass through. This was an effective and sustainable method of salmon harvesting, a method that provided for a controlled fish capture but still ensured that enough fish would get through and reach their spawning areas farther up the river.[28]

The Communal Fish Pot

The main salmon that swims up the ċuumaʕas to spawn is the miʕaat, sockeye salmon, and this is the principal salmon in our diet. In the summer months, when the miʕaat are in season and making their way up the ċuumaʕas to their spawning areas, Tseshaht community members come together every Sunday for a community fishing day. Our community Fish Day takes place at an area on the river known as saaʔaḥi, which is a five-minute walk from where I grew up. Most people refer to this area as the Papermill Dam, or the Dam, named after the mill built there by the B.C. Paper Manufacturing Company in 1894 but shut down a few years later.[29] saaʔaḥi is an ideal fishing spot because many runs of salmon pool there before making their way through the rapids just above the dam and then up the river to their spawning grounds.

Typically, Fish Day begins at six in the morning and ends at noon. When I was young the fishing was done in wooden ċapac, or carved cedar canoes, with one ċapac being used to set the large drag seine net and one or two canoes being used to chase the fish into the net. Two men would be in the main canoe and would set the net, one man releasing the net from the back of the canoe into the water, and the other man paddling the canoe in a circle around the school of salmon. I think about this today and how strong these men were to handle a large and very heavy commercial seine net with just their upper body strength, and the skill and knowledge they needed to catch those fish. By the 1970s the čapac were no longer utilized for our communal fishing day as we began using aluminum and motorized boats, which made it much easier for the men to navigate and manage the large net.

The fishermen had a keen eye for watching for salmon and would know exactly when to set the net. As a young girl, Patricia Jimmy attended Fish Day with her family and tells a story about watching Harry Sam climb a tall tree that was slanted toward the water. He would sit there watching for the school of fish to pool in the fishing area. When he spotted the fish he would alert his brother Pushi (Chuck Sam), who was steering the canoe with the net.

> He would yell, "There they are," and the net would be set. If Harry wasn't up in the tree, he was in the canoe with Pushi. It was awesome when Pushi ran Fish Day. He never used a motor boat, he used a canoe, and while he was setting the net rowing, Harry would be throwing the net for him.[30]

Once the salmon swim or are chased into the right spot by the other fishermen in their boats, the men begin setting the net from a sand bar a few yards off the beach. Community members hold the end of the net while the boat pulls the rest of the net out into the water. When the net is set in a semi-circle, additional community members take the other end of the net from the fishers in the boat and pull it toward a small island[31] where other nets are pulled up to shore. While the net is being pulled in, the fishers circle it and bang on the sides of their boats or throw rocks into the water to keep the fish from trying to escape. The community members who are holding the front line of the net then start making their way along the sand bar and through knee-deep water to join the others on the island. Once they reach the island, both sides of the net are pulled in. The fish that are caught are removed from the net and placed to the side in large tubs or in one of the boats. This communal fishing continues

2.1 Tseshaht Communal Fish Day. *Photograph courtesy of Darrell Ross Jr.*

throughout the morning until an adequate amount of fish is caught, and then it is distributed among the members.

Fish Day is one of my most significant memories of growing up in my community. As I grow older, I have reflected on its continual significance and importance in strengthening our community and familial bonds. It maintains our sacred relationship to the salmon, especially the miʕaat or sockeye salmon. Fish Day brings our community members together, and as a young girl I found it was a time I could spend with my relatives and friends, enjoying the cool morning water as we helped the older community members with the fishing. When the fishing was done for the day, our parents allowed us to enjoy some swimming time before we headed back home to begin processing the fish.

I remember how our elders would take salmon from the first catch to cook for all the community members who were there. The fish would be cut and cleaned and then were ready for cooking. Most of the fish would be cooked by a process called kačas, whereby the salmon were cut in half and then fastened to a large stick with smaller sticks going across the fish to hold it in place. These were then positioned around an open pit fire and cooked on one side, then the

2.2 Tseshaht elders Agnes Sam and Kathy Robinson preparing kačas salmon in the 1970s. *Photograph courtesy of Bob Soderlund.*

large sticks would be turned and the fish would be cooked on the other side. The remainder of the salmon was cut up and put in a communal fish pot, along with the heads, tails, and eggs, and then boiled. Another pot of water would be placed on the open fire for tea.

Once the fish were cooked, the elders removed them from the kačas sticks and took them to wooden tables situated along the beach. Maple leaves were picked by the younger community members and placed by the fish. Community members would get in line and take a maple leaf. A piece of salmon was placed on it by the elders, and if one of the elders had decided to bake the night before, we would also receive a piece of freshly baked bread. A few mugs and cups would be shared and passed around by community members, who would use them to dip into the fish pot and drink the broth, or take pieces of the fish that were boiled. We would take our piece of fish on the maple leaf and find a nice spot along the beach to eat and enjoy this healthy feast. The kačas salmon has a rich savory, smoky taste. In my opinion, nothing can compare to it, especially when the fish has just come straight out of the water.

Family, Community, Reciprocity, Elder Knowledge Transfer

For the Tseshaht, Fish Day has meant more to us than just getting a share of salmon. Although it has changed over time, which I discuss later in this chapter, it continues to be an activity in which our culture and fishing tradition are maintained and strengthened; where respect is upheld and our relationships to our elders, relatives, community members, salmon, and ċuumaʕas are reinforced; and where stories are told and our traditional food is shared—within a context of reciprocity.

Les Sam, now in his sixties, reflects on these early days when his dad Pushi and his uncle Harry oversaw Fish Day and when the elders would feed everyone in the spirit of unity and community. He says, "The first fish always went into the pot and was cooked and shared with everyone on the beach. We ate together, we would eat with everyone."[32] Patricia Jimmy also frames her childhood recollections of Fish Day within a context of sharing, where community members came together to share stories, and laughter, but mostly salmon. Those were "good times," says Patricia, whose favorite part of the day was when the elders cooked the fish and she and her siblings got to eat it on maple leaves. "I loved it when we would have boiled fish or kačas fish cooked over the fire and eaten on leaves. Mmm, so delicious."[33]

Anne Robinson, now in her sixties, places her memories of Fish Day within a context of community and family bonding. "All the people reaped the rewards of being there," says Anne. "It was not just for the fish, but the rewards of being a community, building those bonds, that pulled them together as a family." Anne's mom Kathy was one of the elders who cooked the fish at Fish Day and who has been instrumental in passing down cultural knowledge to the next generation. Anne says, "When I look back on it, for me it was just an example of a way of life where everything is connected. Not in a romantic sense of being connected. Tseshaht Fish Days were about community, family, and sharing"—the communal fish pot.[34]

Anne remembers how when she was young some of the elders would perform rituals in the water during Fish Days. "I didn't know what they were doing back then, but now I do. They were doing prayers of thanks, being thankful for the day, thankful for the water, thankful for the fish, to give thanks first before they go and take fish. This was so important, this gratitude, to give thanks first."

When Anne was a young girl, Tseshaht hereditary ḥawił Adam Shewish would talk to her about what it meant to have gratitude. He would tell her, "You always have to say thank you because everything out there gives us our life." Our part is to be thankful, be respectful and look after them, Anne continued: "That's our part. That's what I see when I look back."[35]

Our Tseshaht hereditary chief Adam Shewish was well known and well respected in our community because he lived his life according to his position as a ḥawił. He was raised with the cultural teachings of sharing and thankfulness, especially around food. Tseshaht Cultural Coordinator Darrell Ross Sr. connects these teachings to reciprocity.

> Back in the day, food was the wealth of the chief. The ability to feed his people, that you had enough food, the process, connection to others. Community members under the chief would bring fish to him and he, in turn, would share it with his people and with others. This built and reinforced community. Sharing was the main aspect. If you couldn't feed your people it meant that your society wasn't functioning. The chief wanted to make sure that everyone was happy. If you had food you always shared it, especially the elders, they always shared their food, even if it was just a cup of tea.[36]

In the summer of 2012, Tseshaht member Janice Johnson interviewed community members for her master's thesis, "Relationship between Traditional Resource Harvesting and Traditional Knowledge Transfer." Community mem-

bers shared their personal thoughts and stories about what this Tseshaht tradition meant to them. Their stories reflect the importance of knowledge transfer,
respect, and reciprocity. One community member shared, "Everyone was like
family when they were in the water together, doing things together so that's
where I learned real lots about family, that teaching that we work together as
family."[37] Another community member reinforces the importance of the knowledge that is shared and gained while fishing together.

> Through experiences such as fishing, this allows members to watch,
> listen and learn, and most importantly the opportunity to gain and
> live respect. . . . the younger ones are always watching so it is impor-
> tant to live by example. It is believed that children become what they
> see and if you live life showing respect then they will most likely do
> the same. Overall, respect is showing appreciation for everything
> that exists on this earth. It is also an act of sharing and giving back.[38]

Patricia, who is now in her mid-forties, reflects back on Fish Day and her
story demonstrates the impact it had on her as a young girl, and how an incon-
sequential detail of that day would have such a profound effect on her. As an
adult, it continues to elicit fond memories. She says:

> There is that one tree everyone drives around before they park. Well,
> my favorite memory is when our family would do this and once
> parked we would be allowed to get out and play. To this day I love
> going for a drive to the Dam just to drive once around that tree. I love
> this memory so much, that I told my son Aaron that when my time
> comes to pass that I want my funeral procession to go once around
> that tree at the Dam before I am laid to rest—this in honor of what
> was one of my most favorite childhood memories.[39]

"We Get a Crap Load Done"

Community Fish Day ends at noon and then the hard work begins, processing
all of your fish. The fish processing continues to reinforce familial and communal bonds with relatives and community members getting together for a day of

smoking or canning salmon while at the same time sharing stories, laughter, cultural teachings, and food. One community member shared with Janice how processing fish was a family activity that brought relatives together.

> Canning is a party for us. . . . There's my family, my mom and dad, my grandma, my aunts and uncles, we all kind of have one big party; we get propane burners to cook the fish. And we just sit and cut fish up, and eat together, and talk, and hang out, and share with each other, help each other. And we get a crap load done.[40]

Processing the salmon brought relatives together and, for me, it was a time that I could spend with my mother Evelyn,[41] listening to her stories as she watched over me to make sure I was doing everything right. I learned how to jar fish when I was ten years old, and it is a processing tradition that I have maintained all of my life. The main processing we did, and still do, is to jar our salmon. We still call it canning, although we do not use cans; we use mason jars. My mum and I would cut up the fish outside in our backyard, and when they were all cut and cleaned, we would put them in a plastic tub and bring them into the kitchen. All our jars would be sterilized with boiling water poured over them. Today most people sterilize their jars by washing them in the dishwasher, but we did not have a dishwasher back then. We would cut the salmon into small pieces with the skin and bones intact, and then place them in the sterilized pint-size jars. We would squish as much fish into the jar as possible, leaving about a half inch of space on top.

My mum would always check and make sure no flesh or bones were sticking up over the top, as this could cause the lid not to seal properly. My mother was born blind and in her teen years she had surgery that gave her 7 percent vision. So whereas most people would check the jars by glancing them over, my mom would use her fingers, gently running them over the top of the jars. If just one little piece of salmon or a bone was sticking up above the jar line, she would make me rearrange the pieces until she was satisfied that they were in the jar properly. I still smile when I think of this procedure. I would have all of the jars done and ready for the lids to go on and then I would hear Mummy say, "No, these ones need to be re-done." I would be irritated because in my ten-year-old brain I thought I did a perfect job. But I would not say anything and would go back and rearrange them while thinking, "Dang, how did you spot that?" To this day, even though I can perfectly well see if anything is sticking out the tops of the jars, I still run my finger over the tops just to make sure, the same way my mum used to do it.

Once my mum approved all of the jars, we then added a teaspoon of salt for taste and a teaspoon of vinegar to soften the bones. After doing that, we would secure the lids and place them in the canners that contained a few inches of water. Back then, we used porcelain enamel-coated canners, and it would take four hours to cook a batch of jars. But as more people got accustomed to using pressure cookers and could afford to purchase them, we moved to this process, which greatly shortens the cooking time, down to ninety minutes. Once the fish was cooked, we would remove the jars from the canner and gently place them on a towel on the table. After all the jars of salmon were cooked and cooled, they would be put into boxes and stored away for future use. Our elders always said that jarred salmon tasted better after at least a year in the jars, so we always had a supply from the year before that was ready to eat. After we finished a day's worth of jarring fish, my mum and I would usually head to the river for a nice refreshing swim before she would begin cooking dinner for our family. My mum passed away many years ago, but every time I jar salmon I think of her and have these wonderful memories of listening to her humming her favorite songs as she shared this valuable knowledge with me, knowledge that I hold dear.

Similarly, Cathy Watts, now in her fifties, was raised with the traditional teachings of learning through observation, especially in learning from elders. She was told by her mother to go watch the elders, to learn how to cut fish and skin deer. Much of what Cathy learned about fish processing came from her mother-in-law Agnes Sam's teachings. Agnes, or Green Aunty, as many community members called her, was one of the elders who cooked the fish at community Fish Day and was well known in our community as a bearer of cultural knowledge, especially foods knowledge. Cathy learned from Agnes how to smoke fish. On her first fish processing day, Cathy was prepared and had her pen and paper ready to take notes on how to smoke fish. When Agnes saw Cathy take out her pen and paper she gave her a bemused look and said to her, "What are you doing? You don't have to write it down—watch."[42]

Agnes was always ready to pass down her cultural foods knowledge to anyone who wanted to come to her home and learn. I have fond recollections of Agnes, or Green Aunty, who was my grandfather Hughie's sister, and how her

2.3 Salmon cut and placed in jars for the canning process. *Photograph courtesy of Charlotte Coté.*

home always smelled like fresh boiled fish, baked bannock, or other intoxicating aromas that emanated from her large kitchen. Green Aunty's home was always open for guests, and she was always ready to share a meal. And not just with humans. Cathy remembers how Agnes would always make sure there was enough food even for the animals in our community. "The dogs would come by her home and scratch on the door, and she would feed them."[43]

Richard Sam Jr., Cathy's son, fondly remembers his grandma Agnes dressed in her favorite attire, a flowing print dress and gum boots, and that she always had a welcoming smile on her face. Richard warmly recalls how his grandma "always had a pot on the stove" ready to make fish soup for anyone who dropped by. What many community members also remember about Green Aunty is what a great baker she was. Her home was filled not only with the delectable aromas of fish or seafood cooking but also the savory essence of homemade pies, cakes, and bannock bread. This was well known in our community, and her older children and grandchildren, as well as other community members, would always stop by for a visit. "And especially at lunchtime," Richard says, laughing.[44]

Eating our foods grounds us to place and reinforces our connections and relationships to our homelands. When we eat our foods, Enrique Salmón writes, we are "eating our landscape," eating the stories, eating our histories, eating our worldviews. Our foods "are more than nourishment; they are markers of identity interwoven with landscapes and culturally symbolic events that occurred on those lands."[45] In *Feeding the People, Feeding the Spirit*, Elise Krohn and Valerie Segrest explain how the unity experienced in harvesting, processing, and preparing traditional foods, and the sharing of meals, are integral parts of Indigenous cultural identity honoring our nonhuman kinfolk that give themselves as food:

> People understood that food is precious, is a gift from nature, and is necessary for our existence. Eating foods in this way helps feed the desire for wholeness within us, and it can be amplified when the entire family participates in a meal together. Individuals can become enriched, as they partake in a fundamental aspect of survival with the ones they love, and the family becomes strengthened.[46]

Sharon Fred grew up in our Tseshaht community but moved to the town of Ucluelet, a few hours' drive away, when she was seventeen years old. She would come to Tseshaht in the summer for community Fish Day to get salmon until eventually, when she was in her thirties, she and her family moved back home. When she was a young girl, Sharon lived in our community with her grandparents, Martha and Martin Fred, and much of the cultural and foods knowledge she holds comes from the teachings they passed down to her. When Sharon was six years old her family was in a terrible automobile accident that left her in a full body cast. She was very sickly as a child and stayed home from school a lot with her grandmother, who used this time together to teach Sharon how to can and smoke salmon and tend the fire in the smokehouse.[47]

Throughout the years Sharon continued to expand her foods knowledge and spent many hours with her grandmother as well as other relatives who passed on their foods knowledge to her. She remembers the time when she was smoking fish with her uncle Daniel. Her uncle said, "We're going to smoke dogs today." Sharon was shocked and envisioned them cutting up dogs into flat strips to hang in the smoke house. She did not realize he meant dog salmon. "I thought we were going to smoke real dogs!" she says as she bursts into laughter.[48]

2.4 Tseshaht community member Linda Thomas cutting salmon for the smoke-house. *Photograph courtesy of Denise Titian,* Ha-Shilth-Sa *newspaper.*

Many of the community members who shared their fish processing stories with me weave their narratives around family and teachings from elders. Linda Thomas, who is in her sixties, grew up in a family with eight siblings. Today she attributes her knowledge and her love of canning salmon to these early teachings. For Linda, learning these skills meant their very survival as a family.

> We all had a role because mom and dad had so many kids in our
> house. . . . Dad fished in the same spot every year, and he worked
> very hard. And he would smoke the salmon, and I would help mom
> can them. It's something I still do today, and I absolutely enjoy it,
> something I find peace and quiet with. . . . If it was not for that fish,
> we would not have been able to survive.[49]

Linda did not have her biological grandmothers in her life because they had already passed on when she was a young girl, so she developed strong bonds with other elders, who shared their cultural knowledge with her. Her family lived next door to Weenuck (Lucy Bill), who only spoke Tseshaht. Linda's parents did not pass on the language to their children, and Linda blames the boarding schools for this; children were punished if they were caught speaking their language. Linda spent endless hours with Weenuck, learning through observation how to collect materials for weaving and how to bake. "I was with her from the wee hours of the morning until late at night, and we would go in her canoe and paddle down the river and she'd get her bull rushes." She also learned from another elder, Hetux (Louise Watts): "I smoked fish with her, I cut fish with her, I cleaned fish with her. And this always helped me later on in years. . . . It was because of all these teachings, from watching and observing my elders."[50]

In her book *The Earth's Blanket*, ethnobotanist Nancy Turner explains how sharing cultural and food knowledge reinforces familial and community relationships and maintains reciprocal and sustainable relationships with the environment that provide us with food.

> Narratives and conversation . . . reveal lessons and ethical approaches to relationships with other people and to the environment. They are a way to share culturally sanctioned rules and protocols that have helped some societies to exist and sustain themselves within their local environments for many generations. Part of their traditional ecological knowledge and wisdom, these teachings are thoroughly linked and interwoven with practices and techniques for sustainable resource use, and with ways of learning and communicating both specific practices and ethical and moral principles.[51]

Linda faced many hardships throughout her life, but she was determined to change, and she credits her survival to these teachings from these women who impacted her life. As an adult transitioning into the role of elder, she feels an obligation to pass on this knowledge. She says, "I want to make a better life for myself, my children, and my grandchildren. I always look back at what was taught to me as a child. To me, that's really important. For me, I always remember our elders. I always believed you can do whatever it takes to survive. I will teach my children and my grandchildren. . . . I want to leave this behind for them . . . to be a role model."[52]

Sharon's health issues plagued her into her thirties, and her doctor finally sent her to an allergy specialist, who tested her and found that she was allergic to many store-bought foods, especially commercial meats. She began to learn how to preserve wild meats, deer and elk, which she roasted, canned, and smoked. She would barter with her fish, exchanging it for wild meat. Sharon was able to overcome her health issues by decolonizing her diet and eating traditional and healthy foods, and she has become an advocate for helping others in our community get on a path to wellness. She shares her foods knowledge with others and invites community members to her home to watch, participate, and learn how to process traditional and healthy foods.[53]

The way colonialism continues to impact our communities is evident in Sharon's narrative about teaching canning to community members and the disruption in knowledge transfer. She was asked by our Tseshaht administration to teach a canning workshop, and Sharon really hoped it would be a community experience. She had ten participants and they canned deer, elk, and tuna. When the food was in the jar and began the timing process in the pressure cookers, the participants said to her, "Now what?" She said, "Now we sit here and talk to each other; you never leave your canning." Half of them left and said they would come back when it was done. But the ones who stayed really wanted to learn and started thinking about how they could utilize this new foods knowledge and can other healthy foods like vegetables and fruit. With Sharon's canning lessons, the community members learned how easy it was to can and preserve healthy foods while simultaneously reinforcing community and knowledge transfer, knowledge passed down to Sharon from her elders.[54]

Sharon, who is now in her mid-thirties, never forgets the wisdom of her grandparents and how their love and cultural teachings profoundly impacted her life. These teachings shaped her attitude toward helping others live a healthy life. She passes on the traditional foods knowledge she received from them to anyone willing to learn. She shared with me a dream that embodies this philosophy of the elders' wisdom and how we are enriched by their knowledge. She says, "In my dream I'm dancing with my grandfather and my grandmother is sitting on a chair watching us. Grandpa is holding money in his hand and waving this money as we dance. The money symbolizes wealth, the wealth in the knowledge they passed down to me."[55]

Fish Day still takes place every Sunday in the summer months, but some community members, especially those in their fifties and older, have witnessed changes that reflect larger societal change, namely through the impact of capitalism on our society. One significant change is that it is rare to have salmon cooked during Fish Day, thus impacting the communal sharing of a meal. Many elders no longer attend Fish Day because they now get their fish delivered to their homes. And while this makes it much easier for the elders, some community members like Anne Robinson see it as a rupture in cultural transmission that took place at Fish Day, with elders passing their knowledge to the younger generation. "The old timers showed us how to live. It wasn't through words, you got to see it; it was part of our teaching. We lost this in some of the generations."[56]

We fought hard for our cultural right to harvest salmon, and as I discuss later in this chapter, we finally won a legal case also enabling us to trade, barter, and sell our fish. While this legal case is seen as a positive reinforcement of our relationship to salmon, it also has brought issues that threaten it. In her thesis, Janice includes interviews with community members who shared their thoughts on how Fish Day has changed, and many of the narratives highlight the issues that Indigenous peoples face living in a capitalist and money-driven world. With the legal affirmation of the right to sell fish, non-Native fish buyers will set up stations close to where our Fish Day is held so that they can purchase fish immediately after it has been caught. Selling, trading, and bartering fish is not something new to the Tseshaht, and many people have sold salmon throughout the years, including my family, using this money to purchase other foods, clothing, and items needed for their families. However, as some community members shared with Janice, having a buyer parked right next to our community gathering place is a temptation for some community members, who sell their fish rather than bring it home and process it. Some see this impacting our cultural values with the temptation of making a quick buck.

> The gathering is still there but the difficult part is to get your fish home because the buyer, the fish buyer is right there from your right hand to your left hand that buyer is right there. And I would say a lot of that fish does not get home.
>
> Yeah, individuals and buyers being close to where the fishing is happening is a bad thing. . . . When I look at how much fish that they get and how much fish leaves with individuals, everybody's looking at it as money now.[57]

In many households both the father and the mother are employed in full-time jobs, making it difficult to find time to bring the family together to process fish.

Some community members therefore take their fish to local non-Native fish processing plants in the nearby cities to have their fish jarred, smoked, or vacuum sealed. One community member shared with Janice, "There are businesses, businesses that will actually do it for you so you pay them to get the canning and smoking done because it's more convenient because nobody has the time anymore. I was a working mom and it was a necessity."[58]

I used the metaphor of a communal fish pot to discuss our Tseshaht community fish day and I still believe that this metaphor fits with what has been maintained over the years. It is still a day and a time when our community members can come together to share stories and laughter, to get out onto the water and immerse ourselves in ċuumaʕas, the Somass River, and to maintain a cultural relationship with the salmon. Yet the world is becoming a place of technology, where visiting a friend or relative is through social media sites rather than physical communication, and as a community member shared with Janice, this makes our community Fish Day that much more important.

> So there is a shift in how people communicate and that's why fish day
> I think is so valuable. Because it brings back like a community spirit
> and a way for people to get together and communicate outside of that
> whole world of technology that currently exists.[59]

Anne Robinson shared this reflection with me, which I think effectively sums up the changes we have witnessed to our community Fish Day: "It's different today. I'm not going to say it's right or wrong, just different."[60]

Challenges to Our Cultural and Treaty Rights to Salmon

The late Billy Frank Jr., a leader in the fight for Northwest Coast treaty fishing rights, positioned food sovereignty at the core of Indigenous struggles for political and cultural sovereignty: "Our treaties recognize that food is at the center of our cultures. Indian tribes are sovereign nations, and part of that sovereignty includes access to the traditional foods needed to keep ourselves and our communities healthy and strong."[61] The Tseshaht, like the majority of First Nations in British Columbia, have never signed a treaty, largely a result of early colonial policies that refused to acknowledge our land and water rights, and we, like other Nuu-chah-nulth Nations, have been involved in litigation over our fishing rights.

After years of frustrating and unproductive treaty negotiations, in 2003, eight Nuu-chah-nulth First Nations initiated a landmark lawsuit against the Canadian and B.C. governments asserting title and rights to their fisheries resources, not only the legal right to harvest the fish in their territories but also the right to trade, barter, and sell fish.[62] In November 2009, successful after a decade of legal battling, the Nuu-chah-nulth won the legal right to control its fisheries. On hearing the decision, Nuu-chah-nulth Tribal Council President Cliff Atleo Sr. declared, "Today this decision confirms what we've known all along. We have been stewards of our ocean resources for hundreds of generations. And the government of Canada was wrong to push us aside in their attempts to prohibit our access to the sea resources our people depend upon."[63]

Legal challenges are one of many problems we encounter in maintaining a relationship to salmon and asserting our right to food sovereignty. Pollution, urban development, pipelines, recreational activities, fish farms, and habitat destruction continually threaten the salmon, threaten our health, and threaten the health of the waters and our homelands. Environmental degradation through water contamination, hydroelectric dams, and biodiversity loss is a key factor in the decline in Indigenous foodways, along with climate change and ocean acidification, which have raised uncertainty and instability in our food systems.[64] Here in the Northwest Coast, especially in British Columbia and Washington State, marine net-pen Atlantic salmon aquaculture is threatening our wild Pacific salmon stocks and the ecosystems in which they and we thrive. Fish are kept in cramped pens, making them susceptible to the transfer and spread of disease. The pesticides and antibiotics used to treat these diseases, as well as food and feces runoff, spread into the open water, threatening the coastal ecosystem.[65]

In 2017 a fish farm pen on Washington's coastline collapsed, releasing over 300,000 Atlantic salmon into the Pacific Ocean. Kurt Beardslee, the director of the Wild Fish Conservancy Northwest, called this collapse an "environmental nightmare."[66] This disaster and the condemnation and concern of Washington citizens and tribal leaders impelled the state government to initiate a process to phase out fish farms by 2025.[67] Prompted by protests over coastal fish farms, especially from the Indigenous communities in close proximity to the pens, in 2018 the British Columbia government announced the phasing out of coastal fish farms by 2023 and established a plan that includes consultation and input from coastal First Nations.[68] In their article "Global Environmental Challenges to the Integrity of Indigenous Peoples' Food Systems," scholars Nancy Turner,

Mark Plotkin, and Harriet Kuhnlein assert: "Globally, all marine systems are now showing deleterious effects of human caused change. . . . The integrity of indigenous peoples' food systems is intimately connected to the overall health of the environment. Recent declines in many aspects of environmental quality, from loss of biodiversity to environmental contamination, have combined with social, economic, political and cultural factors to threaten the health and well-being of indigenous peoples."[69]

Having Fabulous Fish Attire Does Not Make You a Good Fisher!

In 1994 I moved to California to pursue graduate studies at UC Berkeley, and on completion of my doctoral program in 2001, I received a job offer at the University of Washington. I have lived in Seattle ever since. I maintain connections to my Tseshaht community, where I still have a home, and try to go back there at least every other month. I always go home in the summer months when the salmon are running, so I can attend Fish Days and can and smoke fish with my relatives. I grew up canning fish with my mom and I became an excellent fish cutter. Throughout the years I have continued to can salmon, and recently I began smoking fish with my Aunty Marilyn. I used to smoke fish with my cousin Hammy when I was in my twenties, but because I moved back and forth to Vancouver while I was completing my undergraduate education, I never kept up this skill and focused more on jarring fish. Aunty Marilyn and Uncle Rudy built a small smokehouse by their home and offer it to anyone who needs a place to smoke their fish. My aunty learned how to smoke fish when she was a young girl and is always willing to share her knowledge with me and others wanting to learn.

Another fishing tradition I enjoyed when I was in my twenties was gillnet fishing with my sister Gail, a tradition with which I have reconnected in the last couple of years. Along with the communal Fish Day, community members can apply for an individual gillnet license to fish for salmon. My sister and I were one of the first female fishing teams back in the 1980s, and we became quite skilled fishers, although we did have some learning experiences. One of our first gillnet fishing exploits in the 1980s taught us a valuable lesson about river tides and when you should, or should not, set your net. We spent the week getting our fishing gear ready, spending more than enough time on buying our fishing wear ensemble: matching royal blue rain pants, jackets, and boots. We purchased our net and motor and borrowed a fishing boat from my Uncle Porge

2.5 Charlotte Coté with her aunty Marilyn Watts getting salmon ready for the smokehouse. *Photograph courtesy of Charlotte Coté.*

2.6 Charlotte Coté and her aunty Marilyn Watts with their smoked salmon. *Photograph courtesy of Charlotte Coté.*

(George Watts),[70] checked that we had all additional safety gear, and then we were ready to go. We placed the net in our boat and set off down the river, our long hair flowing in the cool wind as Gail confidently navigated us to our fishing spot. We stopped the boat close to where the Alberni canal turned into the Somass River, which is considered an ideal fishing spot, and we began getting ready to set the net.

About twenty feet from the shore was a tall pole sticking out of the water that is used as a marker for boaters, warning them of shallow water in this area. We tied one end of the net to the pole and stretched it out, securing the other end with a heavy weight that we threw into the water. We figured we would leave the net for at least four hours and then come back to check on it and see how many fish we had caught. Four hours later we returned, and yes, we had caught a lot of fish alright, just not in the water. We had set our net just when the tide was shifting from high to low, and as a result, as the river lowered, most of the pole we had tied our net to was exposed, as was most of our net. So there was our salmon, hanging off our net, baking in the hot sun! Tidal shift lesson quickly learned.

Salmon—and a Few Bags of Cheezies

Colonialism and capitalism have put a strain on our communal fish pot, but the fire under it has not burned out. Some of our cultural food traditions have changed, but as is demonstrated by my interviews and interviews conducted by Janice Johnson with community members who still process foods, many Tseshaht members are actively engaged in strengthening and revitalizing our relationships to our foods, and it is their stories that keep alive our hopes and dreams of returning to traditional healthy lifestyles before mamałni, or white settlers, came and disrupted our cultures and societies. Salmon will stay at the core of our cultural identity, providing us with dietary and spiritual nourishment fed to us by ċuumaʕas, the river that feeds us cultural, spiritual, and dietary sustenance.

In 2018 I was able to spend most of the summer back home in my Tseshaht community, and my sister and I decided to revive our gillnet fishing team. Gail has continued to gillnet fish through the years and her fishing partner is her former husband Reg, with whom she has maintained a friendship. I was excited to gillnet fish once again and, much to my sister's surprise, I still had my old royal blue fishing attire from the 1980s. Gillnet fishing opens as the miʕaat, or sockeye salmon, make their way up the Somass River, and when the fish runs begin to enter our territory the day and time are scheduled, usually a twelve-hour opening beginning at six or eight in the evening and closing at five or six in the morning. Most fishers, once they set their net, stay with the net all evening, checking it periodically to remove any fish that have been caught. Gail and I got our food supplies ready—lots of coffee for her and Reg, lots of water for me, salmon sandwiches, a few bags of Cheezies, and a bag of raw almonds.[71]

As the fishing opening neared, we packed our net and supplies in the boat, hooked the boat up to Gail's husband Ritchie's truck, and headed to the marina to launch our boat. Then, along with all the other fishers in the water, we started looking for a good place to set the net and camp for the evening. At first it was fun, like the old days, and Gail and I rehashed stories about our fishing adventures, laughing as we drank our coffee and water and ate some of our snacks. A few hours went by and we began our first check of the net. We put on our headlamps, which help one see the net in the dark, bent over the edge of the boat, and began pulling up the net to check if we had caught any fish. As we made our way along the net, we took off the fish and placed them in a container in the boat. We made our way to the end of the net and then sat down in the boat for another few hours before doing the same thing over again. We pulled out our smokes (a nasty fishing habit), grabbed some more coffee, and then checked Facebook to see how the other fishers were doing.

I had forgotten how extended and tedious gillnet fishing is, and our laughter began turning into complaints as my sister and I got wet, cold, and tired. Five hours into the twelve-hour fishing opening, our conversations about the fun we had had fishing took a turn. I said to my sister, "I'm hungry. Is this all we have for food? Maybe we should phone Ritchie to bring us some more fish sandwiches, or hamburgers." My sister replied, "Well, quit eating all the food. I told you it had to last us all night." A few minutes later I was at it again: "Is this it for the water? I thought we brought another jug." My sister replied, "No, we didn't. I can't believe you already drank all the water. Jesus." A half hour later I said to my sister, "Sis, I need to pee." My sister replied, "For Christ's sake, then stick you bum over the edge and pee." I looked at her and she looked at me and we burst out laughing. I took my pee and we snuggled back down into the front of the boat together and stared out into the calm darkness of the night as the soft waves rocked our boat back and forth. It would be a few more hours before we had to check our net again. At the back of the boat Reg sat, cigarette in hand, staring out at the water, listening to his crazy fishing partners, two sisters reinforcing their love for each other as they strengthened their cultural bonds to the miʕaat, and to c̓uumaʕas—the river that runs through us.

CHAPTER THREE

tuukʷasiił

The Tseshaht Community Garden Project,
Cultivating a Space for Community
Healing and Wellness

M Y SISTER, Gail Williams Gus, has worked as the Tseshaht Crisis Care and Wellness Coordinator for the last eighteen years. In 2014 she applied for and received a $20,000 grant from Island Health's Aboriginal Health Initiative Program (AHIP),[1] which she used to cultivate a vegetable and herb garden in our community. A half-acre plot of land was selected on the grounds of what had previously been the Alberni Indian Residential School (AIRS), a boarding school that was built right in the middle of our community. Gail hired Aaron Woodward, who is married to one of our Tseshaht members and who had some gardening skills, to oversee the planting and maintenance of the garden. Gail and Aaron purchased a garden kit from elders at Tsawaayuus Rainbow Gardens,[2] a multi-level care facility that prioritizes Indigenous residents, who are provided small plots of land to grow vegetables for their community kitchen. "Our first garden was quite simple," Gail says, "with some peppers and kale." They did not have any expertise in cultivating a garden and were astonished at how well the vegetables grew that first year. "Our kale grew three feet high. We couldn't believe it."[3]

At first, many of our Tseshaht community members were not interested in the garden and did not see its health benefits, but eventually some started to come to the garden to help out, bringing compost and seeds to Aaron, who taught them how to plant and weed. Aaron purchased additional plants from other gardeners, expanding the garden from a few rows of vegetables and herbs to two hothouses growing tomatoes, squash, and peppers, numerous rows and raised beds of vegetables with kale, squash, carrots, peas, and beans. They also planted strawberries and an assortment of herbs and eventually added some flowers. The news of the garden spread through the community and more and more people slowly began to come out and help plant, weed, and gather the foods that were grown. With the support of the community members, the garden began to flourish.

Gail, who is in her mid-fifties, has struggled with her own physical health issues; for the last twenty years, she has been dealing with rheumatoid arthritis and fibromyalgia, a struggle that, in turn, has put her on a personal journey toward healing. Although she has days when she can barely get out of bed because she is in so much pain, she continues on her path to wellness and has found strength in our cultural traditions and nourishment in our traditional foods. Both Gail and her husband Ritchie are active hunters and fishers and have worked at creating diets that are rich in elk, deer, and salmon—not just for them, but for their children and their grandchildren as well. As Gail continued on her personal path to wellness she began working with community members to help them improve their own health. She also worked with community elders and traditional harvesters like Nitanis Desjarlais (featured in the next chapter) to learn about traditional plants and medicines.

A garden was something Gail said she really wanted to create as a way to bring the community together, share the foods that were produced, and learn about healthy lifestyles as a way to improve the individual and collective health of our Tseshaht community. The garden became a central feature in the larger health and wellness program she created for Tseshaht members: opening a gym and fitness center; starting a boot camp training program; coordinating workshops on traditional foods and medicines, and on making healthy eating choices; and by helping low-income families in the community create food budgets for healthy eating. Understanding the significance of culture to health and wellness, Gail also began holding classes in cedar bark weaving, moccasin and drum making, and fish canning.

The Tseshaht Community Garden Project, in itself, is an important food sovereignty story about community health and wellness revitalization. The Tseshaht, along with many other Indigenous Nations throughout Canada and the United States, are creating and cultivating community-led garden projects as a way to improve the health and well-being of our members. Tseshaht have been actively involved in maintaining our food traditions like salmon fishing, harvesting seafood, hunting deer and elk, and picking wild blackberries. Indigenous peoples have witnessed the encroachment on our lands and the destruction of our waterways, making it difficult to maintain our food practices and sustain ourselves on our haʔum, traditional foods. Food sovereignty means the right to eat, have access to, and produce your traditional foods, but it also includes the right to healthy foods. Vegetable and herb gardens may not be traditional Tseshaht food, but because of loss of or inability to access many of our traditional harvesting sites, Indigenous people have to find other ways to revitalize wellness in our communities and new ways to re-engage with and revive the relationship with our homelands. Even though these gardens are not exclusively growing traditional foods, they are nonetheless central to decolonization. They help shed the layers of colonialism that have shaped the Indigenous lived experience, and they lead us to engage in decolonizing strategies that work toward restoring our individual and community health, which is fundamental to our self-determination efforts.

For the Tseshaht, and for my sister Gail, where the garden was going to be planted was just as significant as what was going to be planted in it. Once Gail received the funds for the garden, she began planning with the Tseshaht Sports and Recreation Coordinator Tyrone Marshall for where they would put it. They chose the former boarding school site for reasons beyond just gardening. Many of our relatives and community members were forced to attend the school, and many suffered unspeakable physical, emotional, and sexual abuse there. Fortunately, Gail and I were spared that fate. We never attended the boarding school; by the time we were of age, children in our community were phased into the nearby public schools in Port Alberni. I asked Gail why she wanted to cultivate a garden on land scorched by this pain and sorrow, and in a place that triggered memories of anguish and suffering in the former students who went there. Gail responded, "What I saw was that we needed to heal, and the land needed to heal also."[4]

In analyzing colonialism and collective historical trauma, we cannot overlook the disturbing legacy of the Indian residential or boarding schools and the horrific impact Canadian and US Indian education policy had on Indigenous culture, identity, and health. In her article "Intimate Colonialisms," scholar Sarah De Leeuw argues that boarding schools were significant to the colonial project as strategic sites where colonialism was indoctrinated and enacted. In discussing theories of place to conceptualize colonialism, De Leeuw maintains that to understand colonialism, "particularly as a spatialized set of endeavors, it is crucial we investigate the sites and places where it was practiced," because it is in those places "where colonialism's effects were displayed and its tactics actualized."[5]

By the late 1800s, both Canada and the United States had adopted an educational system of boarding schools (also called residential schools in Canada) whereby Indigenous youth between the ages of five and fifteen were taken from their families and communities and placed in these institutions designed specifically to eradicate Indigenous cultural and spiritual traditions, weaken our political and economic systems, eliminate our languages, and sever our children from their communities, kin relations, and traditional foods.

Trauma is deeply embedded in our collective Indigenous experience. However, examining the Tseshaht Community Garden Project through the lens of decolonization and community revitalization reveals how physically transforming this land provides a new narrative for the space, one that tells a story of health, healing, and community empowerment. In reclaiming this land and restoring a relationship with it through sowing and cultivating this garden, the Tseshaht are literally and symbolically decolonizing the space by removing years of historical trauma embedded in the earth and retained in the tortured memories of the former students. In her book *Therapeutic Nations*, Dian Million writes, "Trauma supposes a violence that overwhelms, wounding individual (and collective) psyche. . . . The victims of traumatic events suffer recurrent wounding if their memory/pain is not discharged."[6]

In my research I explore healing in many ways, especially in relationship to our individual and collective physical, emotional, and spiritual healing. I also think through this in correlation to healing the nisṁa (land, earth) and our relationship to it. As Indigenous peoples, we live in a world of reciprocal relationships with the plants and animals that provide us with food, clothing, shelter, and cultural and spiritual sustenance. In return we treat plants, animals, water, land, and air as "gifts" from the Creator, and we are "bound by a covenant of reciprocity," as Robin Kimmerer asserts in *Braiding Sweetgrass*.[7] Decolonization necessitates healing: healing ourselves; healing our nisma; and healing and rebuilding healthy relationships to the land and everything it provides us. In this small but powerful act of decolonization, the Tseshaht community garden transformed a space of pain, trauma, sickness, and death and tuuk̓ʷasiiɫ, cultivated a garden space for wellness, healing, and cultural revitalization.[8]

The Alberni Indian Residential School

Historically, boarding and residential schools were created to support colonization and effectively bring Indigenous people under colonial rule and power. They were seen as effective instruments for the federal government's goal of assimilation. Indigenous children were removed from their homes, families, and communities and confined in these schools for ten to twelve months out of the year, where they were inculcated with Euro-American morals, capitalist values, and a belief in Christianity, while their own cultures, languages, traditions, and spiritual beliefs were attacked and condemned.[9] The US schools revolved around a militaristic regime and many ex-military officials served as administrators. Captain Richard Henry Pratt was the founder of the first off-reservation boarding school in the United States, the Carlisle Indian School, which opened on November 1, 1879. He created an educational system built on the rapid and absolute assimilation of Indigenous children into Euro-American society, which required complete rejection of their own cultural and spiritual beliefs. Pratt's philosophy for creating these schools was clearly evident in his most famous statement, which became the motto for the US boarding school system: "Kill the Indian . . . Save the Man."[10]

In Canada, federally run boarding schools were established following the implementation of the federal Indian Act. In 1876 all laws affecting Indigenous people were combined under one piece of federal legislation known as the Indian Act, which conflated all the diverse Indigenous Nations into the administrative category of "Indian" and created a complex system that administered every aspect of Indigenous people's lives. In 1879 Canadian Prime Minister Sir John A. MacDonald commissioned a study of industrial boarding schools in the United States. He sent Nicholas Flood Davin, a journalist, lawyer, and politician, to Washington, D.C., to learn about the US policy of "aggressive civilization" that removed Indigenous children from their homes and placed them in these schools supported by a militaristic educational regime.[11] Based on Davin's recommendations, Canada created residential schools having less of a focus on military-regimented schooling and more of a focus on a Christian-based education.[12] Religious groups from many denominations were provided with federal funding to operate and administer the schools. Nonetheless, the intent of the schools in both the United States and Canada was the same—assimilation of Indigenous peoples and eradication of Indigenous cultures. This motive was made quite clear by Duncan Campbell Scott, Canada's Superintendent General for Indian Affairs, who stated: "Our object is not to quit until there is not one Indian left that has not been absorbed into the body politic."[13]

Under this US and Canadian framework of forced cultural assimilation, and within a Euro-American/Canadian value system that encouraged individualism, competition, and a belief in Christian faith, Indigenous children were removed (often by force) from their families, their communities, their homelands, and their traditional foods. As tribal societies, Indigenous identity to a large extent is a collective identity, and so the experiences of the generations of children who attended these schools not only affected those students but also resulted in collective trauma framed within a context of loss: loss of family, loss of community, loss of language, loss of culture, and most disturbing, the loss of innocence through the rampant physical, psychological, emotional, and sexual abuse that many children suffered in these institutions.[14] Maggie Hodgson (Carrier First Nation), founder and executive director of the Nechi Institute on Alcohol and Drug Education, was instrumental in creating awareness around mental health issues stemming from Canada's boarding schools. She called the residential school system "one of the most insidious tools of assimilation," which made eradication of Native culture and language "a matter of national policy,"[15] forcing a Euro-Canadian value system on and into Indigenous children, and forcing Indigeneity out of them.

Between 1867 and 1996 over 150,000 Indigenous children passed through the doors of the sixty schools that were opened in Canada.[16] It has been estimated that over 6,000 children died in these schools. While many children died from the diseases they were exposed to and which ran rampant in these schools, poor sanitation, overcrowding, and unhealthy and inadequate food all factored into these deaths. Justice Murray Sinclair, head of Canada's Truth and Reconciliation Commission (TRC), says it is impossible to know just how many Indigenous children died at these schools because by the 1920s the Canadian government stopped recording the deaths as "children were dying at an alarming rate."[17] The TRC was created in 2008 by the Indian Residential Schools Settlement Agreement, which settled former students' class action cases. For six years the commission travelled through Canada to listen to more than 6,000 former boarding school students and document their history. In its final 2015 report the commission concluded that the Canadian residential schools constituted "cultural genocide."[18]

In my Nuu-chah-nulth nation, more than five thousand children were removed from our communities and placed in eight schools throughout British Columbia. Many of these children were placed in the Alberni Indian Residential School (AIRS), which opened in 1890 and was built on lands in my Tseshaht community.[19] Like many residential schools built by the Canadian government, AIRS was deliberately built on top of a hill "to transmit a colonial narrative of Euro-Canadian domination and superiority over First Nations people."[20] The school was run by the Presbyterian Church until it burned down in 1917. The Canadian government reopened it in 1920 and, five years later, handed over administration to the United Church, which operated the school until it shut down in 1973.[21]

AIRS was situated on lands that were part of our principal winter village of ċuumaʕas, which became our permanent village site in the mid-1800s when the federal government took away most of our territory and forced us onto reserve lands established through federal Indian policy and the Indian Act.[22] The school was constructed on 150 acres of land where our large multifamily longhouses once proudly stood. The longhouses were removed by the colonizers, who forced us to transition to "nuclear family" houses. Four buildings were erected for the AIRS administrative offices and classes, and the rest of the lands were used for a fruit orchard, vegetable garden, and pastures for cattle and horses. Though the setting was bucolic, the children did not reap its benefits. They were only used as labor, plowing the fields, cultivating the soil, picking the fruits and vegetables, and preparing them in the kitchens. However, they were not allowed to eat the food from the garden. The food they grew was either fed to the staff as a way to keep costs down, or it was sold to the surrounding mamałni, white settler communities, with the money raised going back into the school. The children, meanwhile, were fed cheap, poor-quality foods like porridge, powdered milk, hard tack biscuits, and the odd piece of fruit or glass of milk, barely enough food to stay nourished or healthy. My uncle Ben David worked in the AIRS kitchen and recalls how children would prepare good, healthy foods for the staff, but they themselves would get tasteless food or "garbage" as he called it.[23] Irma Boss remembers being sick all the time while at the AIRS, which she blames on the unhealthy foods they were fed, as well as on not being given enough to eat in general.[24]

To understand better the impact the AIRS had on our community and the children forced to go there, I want to give power to the voices of the survivors who courageously told their stories in a book published by the Nuu-chah-nulth Tribal Council (NTC) in 1996. In 1992 the NTC organized a steering committee of Nuu-chah-nulth-aht (Nuu-chah-nulth people) and NTC workers for a residential school study and hired Nuu-chah-nulth-aht to interview people who had attended this school. A total of 110 women and men were interviewed, and their honest and deeply personal narratives of isolation, neglect, starvation, violence, cruelty, and sexual abuse became the nucleus of the book.

My uncle Ron Hamilton was one of the interviewers for the study. He never attended the AIRS, but in the book's preface he writes about visiting the school in the 1950s when he was a young boy. Ron's mother Nessie worked there in the laundry, and she would teasingly threaten him with being sent there when he misbehaved. Ron knew children who attended the school and heard their stories of pain and suffering; he thought of the AIRS as "the ultimate punishment," one that he was fortunate enough to not realize. He writes how the school "loomed dark and foreboding," a "prison-like" structure that struck fear into him as a young boy. The large redbrick main building had a fence and an elevated archway entrance with massive front doors with brass trim. He writes how "this heavy brick construction seemed ready to act as a defense against unexpected attacks. Either that, I thought, or the heavy construction was meant to keep people in."[25]

I grew up a half mile away from the AIRS, and when I was a young girl in the 1970s I would ride my horse along the water pipeline behind the school.[26] Sometimes I would stop at the school and peer in through the chain-link fence, staring at these young Indigenous children in the school yard, kids who looked just like me. By that point the school was for Indigenous children from rural areas; most of the students attending the AIRS were from remote villages in central and northern British Columbia, communities that did not have access to the public school system. I wondered then, what did they do to be locked away in this cold and scary prison? A six-foot-high fence was erected around the school to keep the children enclosed. Confinement was a main aspect of these schools and was strictly enforced; students were not even allowed to get close to the fence. Robert Cootes recalls how even if a student was caught within five feet of the fence, "they got beatings and strappings on their hands and on their bare ass" because they had ventured too close.[27]

The students' experiences at the school were framed in violence. Children were beaten for speaking their language or, as one student says, for even "thinking cultural. They knew what you were thinking when you were daydreaming. . . . I wasn't even allowed to think or dream of home."[28] Every action was monitored and controlled through force and punishment. Former student Irma Boss remembers how they would have to stand in line waiting for their meals, and if anyone spoke, "they would just literally grab them and strap them in front of . . . everybody."[29] Robert Cootes says, "They'd generally just beat kids for almost anything."[30] Robert remembers one supervisor in particular who oversaw the dorms in the evening, and if he heard a noise he would "systematically strap everybody in bed, go through the room, just beat! beat! beat! beat!, all the way through the dormitory, he'd beat every kid in the room. . . . They terrorized the kids with violence."[31]

Sexual violence was prevalent in this school as well. Indeed, one of the first class-action lawsuits by former students dealing with sexual abuse was brought forward by students who attended AIRS. The lawsuit was brought against one of the supervisors, Arthur Henry Plint. Many of the students' stories were about the horrific sexual abuse he inflicted on them. Moreover, many also recalled how Plint and the other supervisors would force the abused students to pray after they had been sexually molested. This was the ultimate hypocrisy. He "used to make me kneel down on my knees and ask for forgiveness," Danny Watts recalls. "You know, we'd do this bullshit about, 'oh Lord, we've sinned, and please forgive us.' What the fuck was I doing? I was just a young boy being manipulated by this old man."[32]

Many scholars and former boarding school "survivors" have written about the appalling abuses that the children suffered in these schools, and in the last twenty years the "survivors" of these schools have shared their stories of trauma as a way to heal the pain and reconcile with the past.[33] But it has only been in recent years that we have seen research that connects contemporary Indigenous health issues with the boarding school system and the dietary change forced on the Indigenous children attending these schools. In the schools, Indigenous children were required to eat foods that many had never eaten before, foods such as domesticated meats, cheese, wheat flour, and sugar, and were estranged from their own traditional and nutritious foods. It is not an overstatement to say that their bodies were being colonized from the inside out with Western foods supplanting their traditional foods.

In 2008 Canada formed the Truth and Reconciliation Commission, which was created to investigate former residential school policies and operations and to support former students and their families in their process of healing and reconciliation. In 2015 the TRC report was released, and many of the findings affirmed what former students had already said about the atrocities they faced in these schools, especially the food insecurity and hunger they experienced. The report also revealed that the issue of hunger and inadequate, unhealthy foods being fed to the students was known by the administrators of the schools, yet nothing was done about it. As early as the late 1890s government inspectors visiting these schools confirmed that the children were underfed. In 1918 Indian Agent John Smith, inspecting the Kamloops Indian School, reported his "suspicion that the vitality of the children is not sufficiently sustained from a lack of nutritious food," especially the older children, who needed not only more food but more nutritious foods to nourish their growing bodies.[34]

In 1942 the Canadian government issued its Official Food Rules, the precursor to Canada's National Food Guide. School inspectors travelling to these schools reported that they did not live up to the national food rules. In 1947 the head of the government's Nutrition Division, Dr. L. B. Pett, concluded following inspections of the schools that "no school was doing a good feeding job."[35] This federal neglect of providing Indigenous children adequate and nutritious foods led to high rates of sickness and death in these schools. The total number of children who died will never be known because of the poor record keeping, some schools destroying their records, and the Indian Health Service neglecting to keep records of the children brought to their hospitals from these schools.[36]

Not only did these children attending boarding schools face food insecurity by being underfed and fed unhealthy foods; in 2013 Canadian food scholar Ian Mosby exposed more of the colonial violence inflicted on them. While conducting research on foods and nutrition in Canada in the 1940s he uncovered documents that revealed how secret nutritional experiments had been conducted on malnourished Indigenous children in boarding schools.[37]

These experiments arose from other studies being conducted on Indigenous peoples at the same time to analyze and provide a solution for why these communities were experiencing extreme social and health problems at much higher rates than in the larger Canadian population. The commonly held misconception at this time, which arose out of racially stereotyped views of Indigenous peoples, was that the social dysfunction, poverty, high mortality rates, and serious health issues Indigenous communities were experiencing stemmed from inherited genetic traits in seemingly flawed cultures. A 1946 study, published in the *Canadian Medical Association Journal*, moved the focus away from these inferior culture arguments and linked these social and health problems to inadequate and unhealthy food. The report revealed:

> It is not unlikely that many characteristics, such as shiftlessness, indolence, improvidence and inertia, so long regarded as inherent or hereditary traits in the Indian race may, at the root, be really the manifestations of malnutrition. Furthermore, it is highly probable that their great susceptibility to many diseases, paramount amongst which is tuberculosis, may be directly attributable to their high degree of malnutrition arising from the lack of proper foods.[38]

These kinds of reports led to a series of intensive multiyear studies of Indigenous communities throughout Canada by leading nutritionists, such as Dr. Frederick Tisdall, the coinventor of the infant food Pablum, in cooperation with the Department of Indian Affairs and the Indian Health Services Branch of the Department of National Health and Welfare.[39] In fall 1948 the researchers turned their attention to Canada's Indian residential schools, conducting tests over a five-year period at six residential schools across the nation with close to one thousand Indigenous children selected for the experiments. These research investigations were conducted by trained dietitians working for either the Red Cross or the federal Nutrition Division led by director Lionel Pett.[40]

One of the schools included in this study was the school mentioned earlier in this chapter, the Alberni Indian Residential School that was built on our Tseshaht land. The children at AIRS were fed diets enhanced with Western food products such as milk and fruit, along with vitamin supplements, while other children in the study were given nothing or placebos.[41] Never was it revealed that in order to conduct these studies most of these children were continually fed nutritionally inadequate diets, sometimes for up to five years, with researchers knowingly keeping them underfed and denying them healthy foods as well as certain types of dental care.[42] Mosby argues that these experiments exposed "the systematic neglect and mistreatment of students in these schools," making these institutions into ideal scientific test centers "providing access to a population of chronically malnourished and vulnerable children who, as wards of the state, had little say in whether or not they participated in the study."[43] What Mosby found even more disturbing was that these food experiments were being conducted without the children's knowledge and without their parents' consent.

Nuu-chah-nulth elder ḥawiiḥtuʔis Benson Nookemus attended the Alberni Indian Residential School from 1942 to 1947. While he does not know if he was one of the children who were unwittingly part of the food experiments, his narrative illustrates the constant state of starvation these children were experiencing while the studies were being conducted. Before being taken from his home and placed in the AIRS, Nookemus's daily diet consisted of traditional foods such as salmon and shellfish, foods he never received at the school. His memories of attending the school are narratives of hunger and sickness. He remembers how the children would get one bowl of porridge in the morning and one piece of stale bread in the afternoon. The school had a vegetable garden that the children cultivated, but they were not allowed to eat these foods, which went to the people who worked there. Nookemus says, "We'd get so hungry, we'd steal potatoes and eat them raw . . . it seemed like some of us were always sick."[44] On discovering that he attended a school that was part of these food experiments and that he could have been one of the children purposely starved for this study, Nookemus says, "I feel angry."[45] After leaving the school Nookemus found his dental health began to deteriorate, and he eventually lost all of his teeth.[46]

While the postwar world was becoming more socially conscious of using humans to conduct biomedical experiments and in the wake of the establishment of the Nuremberg Code of experimental research ethics, in Canada, Mosby argues, Indigenous bodies were being used as "experimental materials," and the residential schools and Indigenous communities became "laboratories" that those conducting the experiments could use to pursue their own political and professional agendas.[47]

Many of the boarding school narratives in *Indian Residential Schools: The Nuu-chah-nulth Experience* were collected more than twenty years ago, yet we still feel the impacts of the boarding school system in our communities today, passed down through generational trauma. In discussing the experiences of people who have attended these schools, I have had people say to me, "Why keep focusing on the past? Why not focus on the future?" The answer is simple. First, that's easy to ask if you, or your family, or your community have never faced the violence, starvation, and trauma that our communities faced because of colonization. Second, focusing on the future is exactly what we *are* doing. This book was written as a way to reclaim our history, to empower ourselves so that "our history can have a face."[48] As Dian Million asserts, to tell one's story, to insist on the inclusion of the Indigenous narrative within the larger historical narrative, is "to counter and intervene in a constantly morphing colonial system." Indigenous "experience was pain that had to be historicized and taken into account in the public record."[49] The "telling" helps us heal.

Collective Colonial Trauma

The tragic legacy of the boarding school systems in both Canada and the United States is understood within a concept of collective colonial trauma. Colonial trauma is best described as "complex, continuous, collective, and cumulative with the resulting transmission of compounded trauma across generations."[50] Collective colonial trauma experienced by individuals attending these schools creates emotional, psychological, and spiritual suffering leaving many feeling spiritually, emotionally, and culturally bankrupt. The boarding school as a colonial project devastated tens of thousands of Indigenous people, and many Indigenous communities are still struggling with its legacy. Still, through this healing process of reclaiming that space, people like my sister Gail are working to restore our communities back to their optimum health. We now understand much better the extent to which colonialism took its toll on our health. As I discussed in my introduction, there is a growing epidemic of lifestyle diseases occurring among Indigenous peoples, such as type 2 diabetes mellitus, cardiovascular disease, hypertension, autoimmune disease, and obesity. As I also noted, while these diseases are increasing in the larger US and Canadian populations, they are even more prevalent among Indigenous populations.[51] In addition, as Canadian food scholars Ian Mosby and Tracey Galloway assert, it is now "fairly certain that the elevated risk of obesity, early-onset insulin resistance and diabetes observed among Indigenous peoples in Canada arises, in part at least, from the prolonged malnutrition experienced by many residential school survivors."[52]

In response to these disturbing trends, Indigenous people are actively engaging decolonization and self-determination by reasserting our authority over our ḥaḥuułi, ancestral homelands, and by reaffirming our relationships to the environments that sustained our communities. In the last twenty years Indigenous women and men have shared stories of boarding school trauma as a way to heal the pain and reconcile with the past.[53] Canada's Truth and Reconciliation Commission was created to address the appalling legacy of Canada's residential school system and to provide a forum for former boarding school survivors and families to come together in dialogue, support, and healing.[54] In *Therapeutic Nations*, Million says the TRC signifies that Canada has finally confronted its colonial past, not because it awakened to the colonial violence perpetrated on its Indigenous population but because thousands of residential school survivors were forcing this trauma into the courts for judicial reclamation, calling out both the federal government and the churches as perpetrators of abuse. The TRC was established to heal the colonial "wound," as Million so aptly describes it, and to address the disparities in health and well-being between Indigenous and mainstream Canadians.

> Healing highlights Canada's historical legacy of colonization as it became linked in a direct causal relationship to Indigenous people's contemporary poor health, both physical and mental, substance abuse, suicide risk, and early death, understood as a holistic, tightly intertwined effect. The colonized subject became a trauma victim.[55]

Paulette Regan, director of research for the Truth and Reconciliation Commission of Canada, has forcefully argued that "real truth and reconciliation can only occur when settlers genuinely begin to understand and take responsibility for the legacy of systematic violence and oppression that characterized the residential school system and Indigenous settler relations in Canada more generally."[56]

Healing the nisma

Healing ourselves from the colonial legacy of pain and violence also requires a healing of the nisma, or land, as our health is rooted in our natural world.

The accounts from former students who attended AIRS are stories of pain and suffering, of sickness and loneliness, of sorrow and despair. The Tseshaht community garden has shifted that narrative to one of health, healing, and wellness—reconnecting our cultural roots and identity to that place, to the nisma, and in return, mending it and restoring it to its cultural identity. Trauma not only situates in the hearts, minds, bodies, and memories of the former students of this school; it also festers in the land, with the stench of violence and pain oozing from the AIRS site. Trauma ruptured the relationships we had with the plants and animals that made that nisma our home. It disrupted the passing of cultural stories that were created, shared, and cultivated on this land. Spirits—of children, of plants, and of animals—lived and died there. Historian Suzanne Crawford writes,

> [The] natural world is imbued with spirits that can be found within plants, animals, and forces of nature. The spiritual traditions of the Pacific Northwest are ordered by a worldview in which the cosmos is filled with interconnected relationships. The natural world is sentient and participates in these networks of relationships. Human activity and human well-being depend upon these systems of relationships remaining in balance.[57]

Robin Kimmerer draws attention to the interdependent and interconnected relationship Indigenous societies had with the natural world, one that became unraveled by settler colonialism, forcing Indigenous peoples into capitalist-driven societies whose culture undermined the harmonious, sustainable, and healthy relationships that previously kept our cultures in balance. Kimmerer writes:

> Children, language, land: almost everything was stripped away when you weren't looking because you were too busy trying to stay alive. In the face of such loss, one thing our people could not surrender was the meaning of land. In the settler mind, land was property, real estate, capital, or natural resources. But to our people, it was everything: identity, the connection to our ancestors, the home of our nonhuman kinfolk, our pharmacy, our library, the source of all that sustained

us. Our lands were where our responsibility to the world was enacted, sacred ground. It belonged to itself; it was a gift.[58]

Indigenous peoples are united in cultures that are embedded in and shaped by deep and meaningful relationships to the land, water, plants, and animals that have sustained our communities. The human-ecosystem relationship is characterized as one of reciprocity and respect, where humans do not control nature but live in harmony with it. Restoring the health of Indigenous communities means restoring the health of the land.[59]

The Tseshaht Community Garden Project

One year after my sister Gail started the Tseshaht Community Garden Project, she took me for a tour of the space to show me what she and the other community volunteers had planted. As we strolled through the garden, I thought about this space, the former Alberni Indian Residential School (AIRS) grounds, where children were sent outside the building to play—to play. They never played. The children were always under surveillance, with every action and movement carefully monitored by AIRS staff. The children knew this. They knew that at any moment they could face violence from staff or violence from other children who internalized aggression. Or worse, they could be sought out by the sexual predators who worked in the school. They never played.

As mentioned, Gail and I were fortunate never to attend boarding school. But the generation before us did, and many of our relatives attended the AIRS. Most of them never discussed their experiences, and it was not until the class-action suit was brought forward by former students that our relatives and others in our community began to discuss their experiences openly. Their memories of AIRS are mostly of violence, pain, sadness, loneliness, and starvation.

As Gail and I walked through the garden, we talked about the suffering that our relatives, our community members, and children from other Indigenous communities had experienced in this school. "Why did you want to create this garden?" I asked Gail. "We need to heal," she answered. "The garden will help us heal." We need to heal: four powerful words that are deeply significant in

3.1 (*opposite*) The Tseshaht Community Garden. Behind the hothouse stands the last remaining Alberni Indian Residential School (AIRS) building. *Photograph courtesy of Gail Williams Gus.*

what our Indigenous communities are doing today. "And decolonize," I said. "Yeah, that too," she laughed.[60] She laughed because many people in Indigenous communities do not place their actions in some concept file or neat category; they are doing this work just trying to stay alive—physically, emotionally, and spiritually. The first time Gail and I walked through the garden, I saw it as providing healthy foods for our community; I never thought about it with respect to healing that land. But every summer since the garden was created, Gail has taken me for a tour to show me how it has grown. I have seen how it has flourished and it made me think about its healing properties, not just for our community health, but for the health of the nisma on which it was cultivated.

The following year when Gail took me for another tour, I asked her, "Do you think the land can feel pain? Do you think the land, trees, and plants saw what was happening to the children and as the children suffered, they too suffered?" Gail leaned over and picked a leaf off a huge head of kale and answered, "Yes. The land, the plants, the trees, they felt the pain too."[61]

After receiving the funding for the garden, Gail and other community members began to prepare the land for cultivation. She says, "There was old mud, old soil, not good for a garden. But we thought it would help people, low-income families who couldn't afford fresh vegetables, to let them try healthy foods like squash and kale." At first many community members were not interested in the garden. Gail says, "There were some community members who didn't support the garden. They said it was a waste of band funds. But the money came from grants, not band funds. Some community members said, 'It's going to attract bears.' And I said, 'Our bears need to eat too.'" Gail did not give up, and she made it a point to bring vegetables to community members' houses and give them recipes and ideas on how to eat the foods. She remembers the response of one of the women to whom she brought vegetables. The woman looked at the kale and said, "Ew, I'm not going to eat it."[62] Gail connects this response to boarding schools and the fact that most children in these schools did not have access to nutritious foods and rarely had fresh vegetables or fruit in their diets. Even after leaving these schools, many former students continued to make poor food choices, having lost the cultural connection to their traditional foods and having developed instead dietary patterns with little nutritional value. Despite the skepticism of some in the community, the garden did very well the first year,

3.2 Gail Williams Gus in the Tseshaht Community Garden hothouse. *Photograph courtesy of Charlotte Coté.*

3.3 Tseshaht community members Oswald and Mary Felsman picking kale with their son. In the background is the Nuu-chah-nulth Tribal Council office built on the land where the main AIRS building once stood. *Photograph courtesy of Gail Williams Gus.*

and Gail invited all Tseshaht members to come and check out the bounty they had grown, encouraging them to take any vegetables or herbs they wanted.

Gail gathered the first harvest from the garden and brought it to our community cultural center, where she organized baskets for the elders and filled them with luscious bundles of kale, huge squash, carrots, tomatoes, and other foods. She then invited community members to come to the center and pick up a basket. She was delighted to see a lot of members show up, many of them telling her how pleased they were that she was doing this, and that she was making such a wonderful effort to encourage and support healthy lifestyles and choices.

Gail remembers two women in particular who stopped by for a basket of food. They thanked Gail for their baskets. As they were walking to the door, she could see they were inspecting the food in their baskets with looks of puzzlement on their faces. She asked them what was wrong. One woman pointed to the large fluffy kale on the top of the food pile and said, "What is this?" Gail answered, "That's kale." The woman asked, "What do you do with it?" Gail laughed, "You eat it," she replied. "How do you eat it?" the woman asked. Gail explained to them the health benefits of eating kale and how they could prepare and eat it. The women left happy and enlightened about this new food they were now incorporating into their diet.[63]

I include this story because it really resonates with how colonialism continues to impact Indigenous people's lives. For the Tseshaht, and many other Indigenous peoples overcoming this colonial legacy, it means learning how to be healthy again. Being forced for years to eat unhealthy, overprocessed foods laden with fat, sugar, and salt changes eating preferences as people become more addicted to these kinds of foods, which they then crave, as already discussed. So, it is understandable that these women would not have had any idea what the health benefits of kale are, especially after living in a community where kale is not readily available. By introducing kale to community members, Gail is in effect introducing them to a healthy food and a healthier lifestyle. While we Tseshaht have been actively involved in maintaining our food traditions such as salmon fishing, harvesting seafood, picking wild blackberries, hunting deer and elk, and gathering plants and medicines, loss of our traditional territory has made it difficult to support our nutritional needs with a diet of haʔum. Gail has been thinking about how to incorporate our traditional plant foods in the garden. The garden already has the "three sisters," beans, corn, and squash, which are traditional for other Indigenous peoples, though not traditional on our lands.[64] They have been successful in growing stinging nettle, an indigenous plant, but as Gail learned from working with Aaron and talking with our elders, most of our traditional plant foods grow near the water, and the garden is not near a natural water source. They received camas seeds, this being an indigenous plant that Tseshaht traditionally cultivated, but they are still trying to think how best to introduce camas into a garden environment foreign to this plant, and if doing this would be healthy for the plant, growing alongside plants with which it did not have a relationship. As a sort of compromise, Gail has been taking community members out on plant walks to show them how our traditional plants grow naturally and to teach them how to harvest traditional food plants.

Although she initially received some resistance from older community members, Gail quickly discovered that the younger generation was really curious about the garden. Even though food habits are passed down, it turned out that these kids were more interested in the garden, wanting to eat fresh vegetables. She got creative and began crafting programs to pique the youth's interest and get them to focus on making healthy food choices.

> I started out with the children and had a "movie and smoothie night." We made two kinds of smoothies, one green smoothie and one purple smoothie. They both had kale as the main ingredient but we put berries in one that turned it purple. The kids all chose the purple one because they could see it had berries in it and they really liked it. When we told them the purple one they drank also had kale in it they decided to try the green one and they liked that one too.[65]

The years went on and the garden got bigger and Gail continued to encourage community members to use the garden and to know that the foods grown there were for everyone. She was disappointed, then, when she discovered that the garden had been vandalized. Someone had pulled up plants and destroyed some of the vegetables beds. After this happened a few times, Gail had an idea who the vandal was: a young boy from our community. She says,

> So, one day I saw him walking home from school and I went up to him and said, "Hey, somebody's been destroying the plants in my garden. Do you know who it is?" And he said, "No, I don't know who's doing that." And, I said, "I'll give you five bucks to watch the garden and make sure no one vandalizes it. This is your garden." And he took the five bucks and the garden was never vandalized again.[66]

Gail invited children from the Haahuupayuk Elementary School, which is situated in our Tseshaht territory a few hundred yards from the former AIRS site, to come to the garden.[67] She also invited children from our Tseshaht ṫaaṫneʔis Daycare.[68] The children came and happily put their hands in the soil, pulling up vegetables and sampling foods that many of them rarely or never ate. Gail told

3.4 Gail Williams Gus with children from the Tseshaht taatneʔis Daycare. *Photograph courtesy of Gail Williams Gus.*

me, "I find more young people were into the garden, young people who wanted to experiment with cooking and wanted to learn about harvesting plants and medicines. It's the kids that bring their parents to the garden. They are the ones that tell them when the foods are ready to be picked."[69]

Gail and Aaron continued to add more foods to the garden, which now grows broccoli, tomatoes, beans, squash, corn, grapes, a hybrid blackberry, three kinds of kale, stinging nettles, wild mint, peppermint, kohlrabi, and cabbage. They added raspberries and loganberries to the strawberries that had been thriving since the first garden and were now the most popular food they planted. Community members began frequenting the garden to pick the berries, and Gail was not surprised by this, since many people knew how to jar foods and make berry jam. As explained in chapter 1, it is not easy for many people to pick qaaɫqaawi, wild blackberries, because of limited time with two working parents, or low-income families not having a vehicle to drive to the berry-picking sites and not having the money for gas, or just not having the initiative to continue this tradition. Gail and Aaron therefore found a hybrid of wild and cultivated blackberries and planted it in the garden. She says, "We hope that once community members taste this it will make them want to go out and pick wild berries. My fondest memories growing up were of picking wild blackberries with our relatives. I want this younger generation also to experience that."[70] In September 2018 Gail received a $4,000 grant from Trees Canada, which was used to plant thirty trees, a variety of cherry, apple, pear, hazelnut, plum, and peach trees.[71] "My goal is that those trees will eventually be full of fruit feeding Tseshaht for many generations and even after I'm gone these trees will keeping feeding people and the garden will continue to grow," she says.[72] Gail and Aaron coordinated an unveiling of the new additions to the garden and at this time it received its new name, "Nisṁa," which means "earth" or "land" in our language.

Unlike what happened in the garden that was planted and cultivated by students at the former boarding school, all of the food produced in this garden goes directly to our Tseshaht members. In the book *Indian Residential Schools: The Nuu-chah-nulth Experience*, the statement, "We were always hungry," was repeated throughout the interviews that were conducted with the former students who attended the AIRS as well as other schools where Nuu-chah-nulth children were sent. The Tseshaht garden counters this narrative of food insecurity. Gail's garden continues to grow, and more and more community members use it, coming there to pick vegetables, fruits, and herbs. Community member Shaunee Thomas, who is married to the garden manager Aaron, has been using the garden since it was first planted. Shaunee says, "When the garden first started I would harvest tomatoes and jalapeño peppers. I like picking tomatoes and stewing them and making them into spaghetti sauce. And then I started to pick berries. Some vegetables, like beets, I had never eaten before but I tried them and liked them. I started to use the garden because I wanted to live and eat healthier."[73]

Community member Laura Johnson refers to the garden as "a place where I feel at home."[74] She loves to spend warm afternoons walking through the garden, enjoying its beauty and picking berries and vegetables or whatever foods are available, and then taking them home and creating a healthy meal for her family. This was very important to her because a few years ago one of her daughters got very ill. In 2016 Laura's daughter Autumn, who was five years old at the time, was diagnosed with ulcerative colitis, an inflammatory bowel disease that causes inflammation and ulcers in the digestive tract. In October 2016 her daughter had a colectomy to remove her colon. Laura says,

We spent a lot of time with Aaron and Shaunee in the community garden trying to keep up with an organic diet. [At the time Autumn got sick] we were low-income and access to the garden really helped with the high cost of organic fruits and vegetables. She will have this disease for the rest of her life. . . . Autumn loves fish and seafood and Trevor [her husband] and I both get seafood and especially salmon and halibut, which we preserve every year. But she loves the community garden and loves to go there and pick the fruit and vegetables. This garden has played a major role in her health. It is not just important to her health but is important to the health of our community.[75]

More and more community members are utilizing the garden, some just stopping by to drop off seeds or lend a hand in the weeding and watering of the plants. Gail says summer is the hardest time to get people there because community members are more focused on sockeye salmon fishing. So to try and get more people to come there in the summer they planted flowers throughout the garden, many of them edible, and now more people come to see the flowers, stroll through the raised vegetable beds and the rows of berries, and just take in the beauty of the space. As Kimmerer explains, planting a garden restores the relationship we have with the earth and reconnects us in a partnership of reciprocity and mutual love and respect. If you pull weeds and pick out the rocks, the earth will gift you with a healthy bounty. When people ask her what we need to do to restore our relationship to the land, Kimmerer answers, "Plant a garden. It's good for the health of the earth and it's good for the health of people. A garden is a nursery of nurturing connection, the soil for cultivation of practical reverence."[76] The Tseshaht garden has nurtured the nism̓a back to health, removing the historical trauma embedded in the land and providing healing from these colonial wounds.

This chapter includes many details about the violent and painful legacy of boarding schools, but it is not about doom and gloom, or pain and suffering. The Tseshaht Community Garden Project is a story of hope and possibility. The AIRS boarding school narrative of pain and trauma is thus replaced by a restorative narrative of wellness. We can overcome colonialism, and it will be these small acts of decolonization that will allow us to survive and to thrive. In September 2019 Gail and the Tseshaht Nation coordinated an event titled "Reclaiming Lost Souls of the Alberni Indian Residential School." They invited former students, many of whom had never been back to this site, to return and let go of the childhood trauma they endured as students and to help release the souls of the children who did not make it back home—as Tseshaht elder qiiqiiqiy̓a Willard Gallic Sr. explained, "to set their souls free."[77]

While at the conference Gail told the former students to go see the garden, and many of them did, walking through the vegetable beds to see the place that once held such traumatic memories now turned into a garden providing nutritious foods. After taking a stroll through the garden they went up to Gail and told her how beautiful it was. One woman said that when she attended AIRS, some of the older students would run away to an orchard close by and would pick fruit there and bring it back to their friends at the school. The women told Gail, "The garden and the trees you planted make us happy, and make the souls that were left there happy. They will now be fed."[78]

Gail continues to struggle with her own physical health issues but continues on her personal pathway toward healing. Central to her journey is helping others who are on their own paths to healing and wellness, because she believes that "if you're not part of the solution, then you're part of the problem."[79] Gail uses our Nuu-chah-nulth philosophy to frame her garden project. "I think of hišuk?iš c̓awaak (everything is interconnected) and how everything is wrapped around healthy living. The garden is making people work on their own personal health," Gail says, by tuuk̓ʷasiił, cultivating a space for community healing and wellness.[80]

quuʔičiƛ

*A Conversation with kamâmakskwew waakiituusiis
Nitanis Desjarlais and ńaasʔałuk John Rampanen*

IN 2010 my friend kamâmakskwew waakiituusiis Nitanis Desjarlais challenged her family to stop eating processed, industrialized foods as a way to
decolonize their diets and stop a cycle of generations of unhealthy eating habits that ran in her family.[1] As they were re-Indigenizing their diets, they could
instantly feel and see the changes taking place in their bodies, which led them
to think deeply about not just what they were eating but how they were living.
In 2012 Nitanis and her husband ńaasʔałuk John Rampanen made a major
decision to move their family to Seitcher Bay, a remote part of Vancouver Island
in Nuu-chah-nulth territory, and to decolonize their lives and diets by living off
the grid in a small, 20-by-20-foot cabin that had no electricity and just a wood
stove for heat and cooking.[2] They wanted to live off the land in a way similar
to how their ancestors did before colonization disrupted their traditional ways
of life. The experience—and the challenges they faced while living at Seitcher
Bay—changed their lives. As John says, the venture hit at the very core of their
cultural identity as each of them was quuʔičiƛ, "becoming a whole person."[3]

I don't think that there was really a need to articulate becoming a quuʔas (whole person) in traditional times, because we were born into that way of life.[4] But nowadays we need almost to be reborn or we need to re-establish, revitalize those pieces. And so, I think that quuʔičiƛ refers to the concept of revitalization of Indigenous peoples, who we are. The fact that it's in our language speaks directly to us as Nuu-chah-nulth-aht.[5]

I have met many people throughout my life who have left an impression on me, but none have inspired me like Nitanis, John, and their family. Nitanis is a teacher and practitioner working with traditional plants, medicines, and foods, and an educator in traditional birth and midwifery philosophy and practice. A natural storyteller, she began working in film. Over the years she has produced films and documentaries highlighting the beauty and strength of Indigenous peoples, with a focus on Nuu-chah-nulth language revitalization and cultural teachings and practices. John, meanwhile, is actively involved in Nuu-chah-nulth language and cultural revitalization. After their experience living at Seitcher Bay he committed to learning the Nuu-chah-nulth language and has now become a fluent speaker. Utilizing his training as a linguist, he develops academic and community-based programs on language revitalization, immersion instruction, curriculum, and resource development. His programs provide land-based approaches to language immersion through a Nuu-chah-nulth lens. To Nitanis and John, language is key to revitalizing traditional foods practices, grounding their work in ancestral ecological and foods knowledge.

Through the years Nitanis has shared her harvesting and foods knowledge with both me and my sister Gail, and we have spent wonderful afternoons together gathering berries and harvesting medicinal plants in our Tseshaht ḥaḥuułi, ancestral homelands. In 2013 I created what has become the annual Living Breath of wǝłǝbʔaltxʷ Indigenous Foods symposium at the University of Washington.[6] I invited Nitanis to attend my first event and share her story about living at Seitcher Bay. The attendees were so impressed with her talk that my Living Breath symposium committee invited her back the following year to set up a traditional foods table. She has attended the conference every year since then, sharing a variety of Northwest Coast traditional foods as well as foods from her Cree culture in northern Alberta. Both Nitanis and John have been our Living Breath symposium keynote speakers, and so has their nineteen-year-old

4.1 Nitanis Desjarlais and her Traditional Foods Table at the 2018 Living Breath of wəɬəbʔaltxʷ Indigenous Foods symposium. *Photograph courtesy of Charlotte Coté.*

daughter Kalilah, who, like her parents, is actively involved in activism and is an advocate for the protection and preservation of Indigenous lands, culture, and language. Kalilah is an incredible musician and songwriter who uses music to shed light upon environmental issues, writing and singing about the devastation of mining, oil extraction, deforestation, and fish farms.[7]

The more time I spend with Nitanis, John, and their children, the more impressed I am with how they live their lives. They are Indigenous people who live what they advocate: a life rooted in activism, culture, spirituality, land, and language. As Indigenous peoples, we have had to conform our ways of living to the colonial structures that were imposed on us, but Nitanis and John continue to challenge settler colonialism by grounding their family's lives in Indigenous values, with all of them committed to learning their language; participating in cultural activities of singing and dancing; and all taking part in harvesting, processing, and eating traditional foods and staying connected to their activism. Indeed, it was activism that brought Nitanis and John together. In 1999 they were participating in a political protest coordinated by the B.C. Native Youth Movement, of which both Nitanis and John were members.[8] Nitanis was twenty-eight years old and John was twenty-one at the time. Nitanis shared with me that initial encounter that led to the beginning of their relationship.

> When I first met John there were things that really drew me to him. He's a lot younger than me and he was really quiet, and he was handsome, a quiet, kind of introverted guy. I remember taking him on this journey down to South Dakota. As I was driving, he was explaining to me the concept of decolonization, what that meant. And I was just blown away. I had dated warrior type guys and political type guys, but they never had a solution to what to do. He had it drawn out thoroughly about how we were colonized and that it was both a physical and mental state of colonization. For decolonization, we had to decolonize our mental [realm], the way that we were thinking, along with the physical decolonization. That's what attracted me to him. He was raised in a strong matriarchal family with strong Nuu-chah-nulth women. So, he was not intimidated by my strong manner.[9]

Although Port Alberni is now their home base, they have stayed true to their activist spirits and continue to travel throughout Canada and the United States, standing on the front lines with their children in fighting for Indigenous rights and homelands. Nitanis and John have seven children together, with ages ranging from nineteen down to six years old at the time of writing: Kalilah, Qwyatseek, Nikosis, Chyyah, Halidzox, Tseeqwatin, and Kimowanihtow. Nitanis has an older child, Tanner, who is twenty-nine, whom she had before meeting John. They are also raising three of John's brother's children, Chico, Coda, and Cheveyo.

Nitanis is nehiyawan (Cree), from the Fort McMurray First Nation in northern Alberta, but was raised in Tsimpshian territory in northern British Columbia, the territory of her Tsimshian/Gitxsan father Victor Reece, who was a master carver and storyteller. John is from the villages of ʕaaḥuusʔatḥ (Ahousaht) and qiłcmaʕatḥ (Kelsemaht), which are part of the larger Nuu-chah-nulth nation. Both Nitanis and John developed an activist spirit at a very young age, nurtured by cultural teachings from their elders and relatives. Nitanis comes from a family of strong, resilient women; her nokum (grandmother), Violet Cheecham, and her mother, Cleo Reece, blazed paths in their efforts to honor and uphold the value and spirit of their homelands and people. John was raised in Nuu-chah-nulth cultural teachings. In 1995, at the age of seventeen, he made the decision to enroll at Vancouver Island University (VIU), where he studied decolonial theory, using his own theoretical framing rooted in the ancestral wisdom passed down to him from his elders and relatives.[10] Feeling the urge to stay more involved at the grassroots level of political protest, he left academe and in 2000 cofounded the West Coast Warrior Society, an organization created to confront colonization through social and political protest and action.[11]

Throughout their relationship, Nitanis and John have continued their activism, participating in protests to reclaim traditional sites, and marching to raise awareness for the impacts of settler colonialism on Indigenous peoples and communities. In their pursuit to help empower others seeking to create change, they focused their attention on Indigenous youth. John created grassroots gathering throughout British Columbia, taking young Indigenous boys and girls out to their traditional territories sometimes for weeks at a time to reconnect to their homelands and the spirits of their ancestors. As Nitanis had more children she learned traditional midwifery practices and healthy living for mothers and their babies. As her family grew, this led her to thinking about ways to nurture the next generation of Indigenous youth by promoting health and wellness through the revitalization of traditional foods and medicines.

Nitanis continued developing her knowledge of Indigenous plants and medicines and began reading lots of books and talking to elders. In her personal journey to learn more about Indigenous foods, in 2008 Nitanis joined the Vancouver Island and Coastal Communities Indigenous Foods Network (VICCIFN), an organization made up of food harvesters and gatherers, health professionals, community development workers, and members of the scientific community devoted to building collaborative networks and approaches in addressing issues such as food security and traditional food access.[12] It was at a VICCIFN conference in 2008 when Nitanis and John started thinking about decolonizing their diets. The conference, Nitanis says, was very science based, with academics talking about the contamination of traditional food. However, something struck her as odd about the conference. While there was a lot of talk about traditional foods, there were no traditional foods there. This made her think about the foods she and her family were eating.

> I realized I didn't really know a lot about traditional foods. I thought, "How am I going to learn about traditional foods without eating them?" And so, we talked about a traditional foods challenge, to live off of traditional foods. I wondered if we could do it. So, we said, "Let's do this. We would have to eat these foods!"[13]

Nitanis began thinking about how they would do this, what kinds of traditional and non-traditional foods they would eat, and how they would focus on an Indigenous trade and barter system to acquire these foods, rather than using money to purchase them. Some non-traditional foods would remain in their diet. Coffee was on their list of non-traditional foods they would still use; milk was not. "I thought, I need cream in my coffee. How can we get cream? Oh, I could use my breast milk," she says laughing.[14]

Decolonizing Their Diets

Nitanis has a long family history of diabetes and unhealthy food choices. Her dad Victor lived with diabetes for thirty-five years; her grandmother, Victor's mom, also died from diabetes. Nitanis's memories of her grandmother are of her always making bread for her family, which her dad loved to eat. Nitanis says, "She would put it on the table and give it to the family. She loved to do this, to give her family this homemade white bread with homemade jam. And he always equated this with love. When dad was in the hospital, he would sneak away to eat white bread. I would take it away and make sure he had smoked fish and oolichan grease and seaweed and stuff."[15] In October 2010 Nitanis's dad passed away at the age of sixty-four from complications of diabetes. That fall, on National Diabetes Day, Nitanis, John and their children began their Indigenous Foods challenge—and took it very seriously. She says:

> I learned from my dad's death. When you give sweets to children, it's usually given like a reward. We can't use these kinds of foods as a reward. . . . If we didn't change our food habits, we would die. If you look into our history there is a connection of foods and colonization and of genocide in terms of food. Colonization forced us away from our foods, which were replaced by processed foods like bannock filled with flour, salt, and sugar. This was part of the genocide; it was killing us. So when we started our challenge it was quite somber.

Nitanis wanted her children's experiences to be different than her father's and wanted them to be raised on haʔum, traditional food. She wanted their memories to be of their mom making dried fish and eating oolichan grease. So she told her kids, "We have to do it. They were in it. They took it on." And so they began their traditional foods challenge. The first day of their challenge they ate local traditional foods, the second day they ate non-traditional foods, and the third day they ate a hybrid of Indigenous and locally sourced, healthy foods. As Nitanis incorporated more haʔum into her family's diet, she began to see how their views and their connection to the foods they ate began to shift.

> The first day was all traditional foods, the second day was colonizer's foods, and the third day was a hybrid of Indigenous foods and other healthy foods. So the first day was ťuċup and ḥaaỷištup [a variety of seafoods] and . . . of course, salmon and halibut, and mussels and clams and crab. Then the next day they had the colonial foods, and it was hotdogs and chili and Caesar salad. [My children] never thought of these before as colonial foods but thought of them as just regular foods. The first day [after eating traditional foods] they wanted to share songs, but nobody got up to share a song for the hotdogs. It was not song worthy. My kids began to feel a spiritual connection to their [traditional] foods.

Throughout the winter Nitanis, John, and their family continued to live on traditional foods, and during that time Nitanis had her sixth child, a daughter.

When they started the challenge, she was fifty pounds overweight. During her pregnancy, while eating mostly traditional foods, Nitanis began to feel positive changes taking place in her body. She did not gain any weight during her pregnancy; in fact, she lost weight and could not believe how healthy she felt by making these changes to her diet and eating traditional foods. Nitanis laughs, "We call her my Indigenous baby."

Nitanis bought an electric smoker, a dehydrator, and a pressure cooker and learned how to jar and process traditional foods as she continued to eliminate non-traditional foods from her cupboard. Her Cree family from northern Alberta also helped out with the challenge; her aunty Kathy sent moose meat so that the family could incorporate foods from her Cree culture into their diet. Their relationship to foods continued to change, and they began to see and feel the spiritual connection to their traditional foods with each meal "deserving of a prayer." Nitanis continued her knowledge gathering, learning about Northwest Coast edible plants and the seasons in which they grew. She cooked a lot of locally harvested salmon and seafood as well as goose and duck. "With chicken and other colonial foods," Nitanis says, "you don't have this cultural connection. I don't know where chicken comes from . . . when you buy these packaged foods there is really no spiritual connection or soul to what you are eating."

It was not just their diets and the way they felt connected to traditional foods that had changed. As Nitanis, John, and their children continued to Indigenize their diet, they began to experience a new relationship to the lands where they were harvesting traditional foods. Nitanis first experienced this when she and her children were out gathering wild berries. As they were picking she started to think about the seasonal changes and when berries grew, and to look really closely at the land that provided these traditional coastal foods. "It was like I was rediscovering the coast for the first time and in a new way," says Nitanis. She began to feel a transcendent peace and an intimate connection to the landscape.

> When I came home with a handful of berries and gave these to my kids, I felt like that was the most real thing I could ever do, rather than go to work and buy food for them. I started feeling a meditative peace when I was berry picking. I felt honored. These berries are growing for me, we are a part of the land. We are stewards of the land. What does sovereignty really mean? We use this word a lot as activists, but what does it mean? To me, this is what sovereignty

meant. . . . This is hišukʔiš ċawaak [everything is interconnected], being able to be out there surrounded by everything, and knowing that these berries were going to feed my children.

Living as Nuu-chah-nulth-aht: The Move to Seitcher Bay

Seitcher Bay is located in one of the many inlets and the many small islands that form Clayoquot Sound on the west coast of Vancouver Island, the traditional homelands of John's people, the ʕaaḥuusʔatḥ (Ahousaht), and the ƛaʔuukʷiʔatḥ (Tla-o-qui-aht) and ḥiškʷiiʔatḥ (Hesquiaht), all part of the larger Nuu-chah-nulth nation.[16] It is a forty-five-minute boat ride from the closest urban center, the city of Tofino, a tiny town with fewer than two thousand residents. It is a twenty-five-minute boat ride from Ahousaht, which has a population of roughly twenty-two hundred, mostly tribal members. By this time Nitanis and John had made their decision and they had already moved their family from Port Alberni to the much smaller town of Tofino to live in a more rural setting. In the summer of 2012 Nitanis was back in her Cree territory in northern Alberta visiting her mother when she received a phone call from John, who was back in Tofino with their children. John said, "Nitanis, let's move to Seitcher Bay." Nitanis thought, well, their house lease was coming up that fall, a good time for them to "jump off the grid," so she agreed. "I was so excited!" They both quit their jobs and began preparing for their new life.

The couple had two months to prepare for their move. John went ahead of Nitanis with their three older children and his nephew to get the cabin ready and to start chopping wood for the damp and chilly coastal winter months. Nitanis stayed behind and began canning and jarring all the foods they had in their freezer, both traditional and non-traditional foods, doing this so that they would have a variety of foods to start with as they harvested the haʔum around Seitcher Bay. Nitanis says, "Being able to feed ourselves and heal ourselves was a big part of this challenge." She felt good about the knowledge she had gained around traditional medicines and how this would benefit them while living in such an isolated location.

When John was growing up, Seitcher Bay had been a favorite summer vacation spot for his family. It was named Seitcher Bay after John's mother Charlotte's family name. John's extended family regularly visited Seitcher Bay, enjoying this connection to their traditional homeland. But gradually, over the years, his extended family members became too busy and rarely visited the area, until only John and his dad still made regular trips. John's father Kalevi, who passed away in 2018, loved Seitcher Bay. When he retired, he would stay there for long periods in the summers and eventually began building cabins for his family and other relatives to enjoy. Nitanis and John chose to marry there in 2004, and in preparation for their wedding, they began clearing the area of bushes. John also helped his father with the building construction. Initially they wanted to build a traditional longhouse, but eventually they settled on building four small cabins, the largest being 20 feet by 20 feet. There is no electricity at Seitcher Bay, and they had no heat source other than a wood stove.

As John was getting the cabins ready for their move and Nitanis was processing foods to take with them, they had to figure out exactly what to bring to Seitcher Bay, and how to get it there, since they did not even own a boat at that time. They began going through their material goods. Seeing how many material things they had accumulated made them think about their practicality. They told their children, "If that's not biodegradable, you can't take it."[17] They narrowed down their material goods to one boat load. Since they did not own a boat they chartered one, loaded it up, and John and their three older children and his nephew headed to Seitcher Bay, while Nitanis stayed with the younger kids and continued to prepare foods. It was a typical stormy, rainy and windy fall day, causing huge wave swells as they made the forty-five-minute trek through the cold, choppy waters. John remembers the look on the boat operator's face when they arrived at Seitcher Bay. "We unloaded everything on the dock and the boat operator was looking at us like we were crazy. The dock was just pounding up and down like a big giant surfboard with our few possessions on it, mostly food."[18]

They removed all their supplies from the chartered boat and put them on the dock, and John went to get a rowboat they had at Seitcher Bay to transfer their goods. When he got back to the dock he saw that the giant waves had rocked the dock and spilled into the water most of their supplies and food, which had sunk to the bottom. But he and his children wasted no time figuring out how to retrieve the food. John says, "I rigged up fishing lines with magnets and gave them to our children. They put the lines into the water and aimed the magnet at the top of the cans. Once it connected, they were able to lift the cans to the dock. What could have been a disaster ended up turning into a fun activity for

4.2 John Rampanen with three of their children and his nephew waiting for the boat to take them to Seitcher Bay. *Photograph courtesy of Nitanis Desjarlais.*

the children, who had a great time fishing for the canned goods." The storm had soaked everything they owned, so the first thing they needed to do was dry everything out. A week later, John went back to Tofino and purchased a boat.

A few months later Nitanis and their three younger children joined John and the other children, and they settled into their one-room cabin, with their oldest daughter, Kalilah, who was twelve at the time, taking one of the other smaller cabins a few yards away. Nitanis made sleeping sections for the kids with curtain dividers. They did this, she says, "so that they had their own sleeping areas. Everybody had their own little tent they could crawl into." They bathed in the ocean when the weather was nice, which they all enjoyed even though the water was very cold. When the weather was stormy they heated rocks in a pot on the wood stove and then put the hot rocks in a large tote filled with water, which they would use to bathe. They had a toilet, which Nitanis's oldest son Tanner and John's father had installed fifteen years before; it filtered into a hole and used a natural process of decomposition.

They also had a good supply of foods that Nitanis had jarred, smoked, and dehydrated, which they ate along with the haʔum they gathered and harvested.

Although Nitanis jarred non-traditional foods such as hamburger, chicken, pork, and other things the kids liked, she wanted to do this because she did not know what kinds of foods they would be able to harvest at Seitcher Bay, if they would have enough food, and if their children would even like these foods. As their supply of non-traditional foods dwindled, Nitanis would refill the jars with harvested haʔum, such as salmon, cod, prawns, oolichan, and a variety of berries. She smoked oysters, clams, and mussels and used both the stove in the cabin and an open pit fire to cook the foods. John set prawn and crab traps and they always had a good supply of cod. To ensure they would not get tired of eating the same foods, they began getting creative in how the foods were cooked, alternating between boiling, smoking, and barbequing foods on the beach. They harvested many varieties of seaweed and sea lettuce as well. Nitanis would mix the seaweed with a bit of sesame or olive oil and some garlic and would flatten it between two hot cast-iron frying pans, and the children would eat it like chips.

Their children adapted well to their new life and to the assortment of new foods to which they now had continual access. Indeed, they became quite proficient in their abilities at harvesting and processing these foods. The boys especially loved to fish and became quite skilled at both fishing and cleaning the fish they caught. They also loved to dig for clams. Nitanis remembers how when the tide was low, the boys would all go out with a bucket and gather clams. "They just loved that."[19] Their daughter Chyya, who was five years old at the time, mastered the skill of shucking clams and oysters, a skill that requires the use of a very sharp knife, which, as John says, they as parents found unsettling at first, but they had to understand it within the context of what they were doing. "In most situations, especially in town, you give a child a knife or a tool like that—you would be extremely cautious, and most people would not do it. Out there it was different. We understood how careful we had to be, especially because it was just us. For fishing and hunting, processing the foods, making the fire, everyone had something to do, with all of us contributing."[20]

John says the experience had unexpected benefits, making them really come together and work on their family. It reinforced their family unit and made them appreciate what he defines as "the essence of being together." Their children got to develop their own unique characteristics, personalities, traits, and skills. Nitanis and John began nurturing their children's individual skills, helping them contribute where they felt the most comfortable contributing. John says, "We honored that uniqueness and diversity in each other. In town, it's different, it's

4.3 Kalilah Rampanen with the lingcod she caught. *Photograph courtesy of Nitanis Desjarlais.*

4.4 Nitanis and daughter Kalilah plucking ducks. *Photograph courtesy of Nitanis Desjarlais.*

not the same. We learned from that. We [he and Nitanis] are the caretakers and providers, the ones that are supposed to know everything. But out there we all learned simultaneously. We were all going through the same experiences."

As they all continued to learn and experience this new life together, their relationship to the haʔum they were eating also changed, similar to what they had experienced while doing their traditional foods challenge a few years before. But, John says, in Seitcher Bay, it was that much more profound.

> When we all put food on the table, it put that much more value to it. We all harvested, and hunted, and grew foods. They have a different value behind them . . . the spiritual aspect. When you eat fresh [natural] foods you are ingesting that spiritual energy too. If the food is heavily processed, you lose that essence. If it's completely modified, it does not have anything. We found also that eating that food we required less, the clams, the fish, they went much further. We thought we would need to get a lot of food because we have such a big family, but you get full off of a much smaller meal of really nutritious food packed with protein and packed with vitamins.

Their oldest child, twelve-year-old Kalilah, became quite skilled at driving their boat and with helping her dad chop wood. She had always loved their family's summer visits to Seitcher Bay, and she thought this would be similar, where the children would be down at the beach or in the water swimming. "I thought this was going to be awesome," Kalilah says. "But it was a lot of work. I was the oldest and I was always helping my dad with firewood every day. There was actually hard work every day. But it was good. I was happy."[21]

Before they left Tofino, Nitanis and John had set up a homeschooling program for their six children with Oak and Orca, a program designed to teach through a holistic learning experience.[22] They had bought books and brought these with them, creating a curriculum that included science, social studies, and math and that structured their grade levels. But as they were teaching their children, they started to realize something. Nitanis says, "I started with 'Okay kids, we're going to do math and this is going to be your education, and then we realized, this is bizarre. It didn't fit." Nitanis and John started to grow more of an appreciation for and confidence in what their children were learning outside on their own. That was more important than anything they were attempting to

4.5 Nitanis and John's children Qwyatseek and Nikosis cutting fish. *Photograph courtesy of Nitanis Desjarlais.*

teach the children with this homeschooling program and with the books. Nitanis added: "The kids unschooled us."[23] Their children's education, John says, was in the very things they were doing on a daily basis:

> I don't think that we were really paying a lot of attention at first to the actual education that was happening on a day to day basis, right. We were harvesting food, preparing it, preserving it, building, going out and getting materials and then making something out of it. All of those were very hands-on educational experiences. And we started to appreciate more and more the educational value to those pieces that they were already doing naturally on a daily basis.

Kalilah, a budding musician at the time, grounded her music in environmental issues and her experiences spending summers at Seitcher Bay. At eleven years of age she wrote a song about čitaapi, the Nuu-chah-nulth name for Catface Mountain, a mountain close to Seitcher Bay, to create awareness about a mining project there. čitaapi is sacred to Nuu-chah-nulth, a place where people went to pray. While living at Seitcher Bay Kalilah wrote "Wild and Free," a song about the environmental degradation produced by fish farms, especially those on the west coast of Vancouver Island.[24] Nitanis said she could see her daughter's music begin to mature, something that Kalilah, even at her young age, wanted to improve. "People would say, 'Oh, she's so cute. And she's only 11.' Kalilah didn't want anybody patting her on the back for being little; she wanted it for being good."[25]

Shedding Colonial Norms

In addition to acclimating to their new environment and way of living, Nitanis and John were also cognizant of the colonial way of life they brought with them, and this became part of their learning experience as they began to shed these "colonial norms." John said they first noticed this when relatives came to visit them. After the visitors left, they had a pile of garbage—bottles and plastics—that they then had to take out to Tofino. This made them more conscious of their own waste and wastefulness, and they started limiting what they brought back to Seitcher Bay from the cities, especially plastic items. They decreased their waste significantly down to mostly paper, which they used for fires.

But this rethinking also made them understand how sometimes it was unavoidable to use and have colonial objects in their daily lives, things like a motorized boat, motor oil, a chainsaw, a generator, and propane for the generator. "These," says Nitanis, "were the comforts of colonial life that we brought to the bush. We did cause damage, damage to the ecosystem with us parking our boat here, the sound of the motors, the motor oil. We did leave an imprint." But as John points out, "In looking back and in hindsight, these things were unavoidable. We didn't have the capacity to be out there without a motorized boat."[26]

The Marten Invasion

Several months into the lifestyle change, John ended up having back issues and pinched a nerve from the daily wood chopping and heavy lifting he was doing. The family decided to go back to Port Alberni and stay with John's mother Charlotte until his back issues improved. They stayed at Charlotte's home for a month and then made their way back out to Seitcher Bay. They docked their boat and headed up to the cabin with new supplies they had picked up in Port Alberni. When they opened the door to their cabin they found that martens (members of the weasel family) had overtaken it while they were gone, having figured out how to move the shingles on the roof and make a hole big enough to climb in. Kalilah says the first thing they experienced when they opened the cabin door was a very odd smell.

> It was kind of weird, a musky smell. It was just quite bad. We turned on the generator and we saw the floor covered with marten shit. Just a whole bunch of little piles everywhere. So, they moved in. Before we had had field mice. [The martens] came and ate all the field mice, and now we were overtaken by martens. Martens have razor sharp teeth and they bit into all our totes. And they went behind some of our [glass jars filled with salmon] to push them, to knock them off the shelf, to break them so they could eat the fish. It was awful.

The martens also took over Kalilah's cabin, focusing their attention on her chest of drawers. She says, "I went to my room in my cabin and they created like a little marten hotel and they used my top drawer as a bathroom. In the middle one they had made little nests and they would bring in stuff. And the bottom drawer they used for food storage. For weeks I was finding like seeds in my pockets. They were living the high life for a while."

Although Kalilah's cabin was also taken over by the martens it had less damage, and fewer feces than the main cabin, so Nitanis and John kicked out the squatters, moved their own family in, and began the cleaning process. They took everything off the walls and off their shelves and washed things down; they picked up all the carpets and disinfected them. When they finally had everything cleaned, they moved back in. The martens still hung around and at night they would climb on the roof of the cabin and poke their heads in through a hole in a tarp that John had secured over the roof. Nitanis was pregnant at the time, and her pregnancy caused her to get up frequently in the night and go to the bathroom. She used this to her advantage. "So, when the kids were sleeping and I was getting up to go pee, I would use a poking stick and I would literally catch them peeking [through the hole in the roof] and I'd poke them, and then they would scurry off."

Nitanis said it was not unusual to have animals in and around their cabins, and they got used to hearing the field mice scuttling around the cabin. Of course, they kept an eye on the martens to prevent them coming back in. One night as she was lying in bed, Nitanis heard a *thunk* right beside her. She turned over to grab the flashlight, and there beside her were giant carpenter ants that were coming in through the roof and, much to her horror, dropping down on her bed beside her. "And I was like, oh my god! Oh my god! Don't get in my hair," she says, laughing.

Black bears also visited their cabin site, but for the most part, John said, they were harmless and left him and his family alone. "You can tell when you have that cohabitation with them; you get to know their personalities. And most of them, they'll keep their distance. You make a bit of noise and they'll look at you—they might not go scampering off right away, but they'll keep their distance and they'll keep an eye on where you're at. And you do the same with them." They eventually got to know the bears and developed a relationship of respect with them. There was one bear that came to their cabin site frequently. They named him Ninja, and Kalilah says he would come to the patio and eat their dog Romeo's food. One morning they opened the cabin door and saw that their tote filled with fish had been turned over and the fish were scattered on the ground. They figured it had been Ninja, Kalilah says, because only one salmon had been taken, the smallest one.

But there was another bear that kept coming around and John said it acted differently than the other bears: "You could tell just in the body shape and the mannerisms that it was a fighter. You could just tell in the way that it behaved it wasn't scared at all, it wasn't startled. It didn't respect boundaries." Worried about his young children, John had to make the decision to shoot the bear. He got a jar of rancid pulled pork that his nephew had brought to the cabin when they first moved out to Seitcher Bay and set it out as bait, close to the beach, where it would be easy to process the bear once it was shot. A little while after he set the bait, the bear came sauntering along the beach close to where it had been placed. As John lined up his rifle and got ready to shoot, a boat filled with tourists came zooming into the bay close to the beach where the bear was standing. The operator stopped the boat, and all the tourists began happily taking photos of the bear while John stood and watched them thinking, "Well, next time when they come by, I'll be skinning it." When they left, John shot the bear and he and Kalilah began cleaning it and removing its fur. As their daughter was skinning the bear, Nitanis asked her, "What does it smell like?" Kalilah replied, "It smells a little like ɫućup (sea urchin) and salal berries." They were unable to eat much of the bear meat because the animal had just come out of hibernation and was very lean. "We ate a little bit," Kalilah says. "It was all muscle. It was pretty tough."

What Do You Bring to High Ground When You Receive a Tsunami Warning?

On January 5, 2013, the Northwest Coast was hit with a powerful 7.5 earthquake along the coastal fault line 100 kilometers west of Craig, Alaska, and approximately 300 kilometers northwest of Prince Rupert, British Columbia. A tsunami warning was issued for the entire British Columbia coastline. That evening, Nitanis and John were listening to the radio and they heard about the earthquake. Nitanis's mom, Cleo, who was visiting them from northern Alberta, was relaxing on their bed.

Nitanis turned on their VHF radio and could hear messages from the Nuu-chah-nulth community of Ahousaht (approximately 10 nautical miles away) conducting a tsunami emergency action broadcast, telling everyone to get to higher ground immediately because of the threat of a tsunami. John, who was experiencing severe back pain at the time, turned to Nitanis and said, "Get the kids, get the kids!" Nitanis's mom jumped up and began putting the children in their winter jackets and pants. When all the children were bundled in their warm clothes they rushed out the door. Nitanis's mother was the last one out of the cabin. Nitanis looked back at her. In their haste, her mother grabbed the first thing that was closest to her. Nitanis laughs as she recalls the image of her mom running out of the cabin door: "And so she grabs a duvet, a giant duvet, and she's got it on her shoulders, and holding a pair of socks."[27]

It was pitch black outside and they began running up a mountain with an injured John in the front holding a flashlight to guide the way. They found their way to an old logging road and decided that was high enough. It was a chilly January evening, and indeed the large duvet that Nitanis's mom had grabbed came in handy. Nitanis says, "It was cold. My mom—thankfully she brought the duvet. We put down some ferns and made an area where we could sit on some alder logs. John started collecting branches to start a fire." And then they sat in the dark and they waited, hearing only the calm sounds of the ocean waves and the soft howling of wind. Kalilah kept a sense of calmness as she thought about how they could survive if the tsunami waves hit Seitcher Bay. "If a wave came we could go get all the food, get the jars that survived," Kalilah reasoned. All they had with them was a wind-up AM/FM radio, which John kept monitoring. Once they heard that the tsunami warning was lifted, they got everyone ready and headed down the mountain. John says he does not recall how long it took to get up the mountain, but he remembers that it took two and half hours to get back to their cabin.

This frightening experience made John and Nitanis think about their pre-paredness if they were faced with another tsunami warning. The next day they began clearing an emergency path by a nearby mountain and created rope railings to hold on to along the steeper areas. At the top of the mountain they buried a large container with matches, dry wood, and jarred food. The children chipped in with the preparation and made a small shelter. Doing this really alleviated a lot of anxiety for Nitanis and John with the understanding that, as Nitanis said, "We can all take care of each other."

The Sea Is Relentless

Many of the challenges Nitanis, John, and their family faced came from the ocean, which they needed to learn how to navigate it in order to survive. Many times when they were in their small eighteen-foot aluminum boat driving from Seitcher Bay to Tofino they faced stormy weather conditions and turbulent water as they made their way through the unpredictable sea. One time they were leaving Tofino heading back to Seitcher Bay. They had loaded up with supplies in their boat, which had not been working properly and was running on only half its cylinders. It usually took forty-five minutes from Tofino to Seitcher Bay, but they had not factored in the heavy load, and their little boat struggled through the choppy ocean waves. John realized it was going to get dark before they reached their dock. As they watched the sun go down they continued, maneuvering through the small islands along the jagged coastline.

John's nephew Joel had a flashlight, but it did little good; flashing light off the cascading whitecaps and sea foam only made it that much more difficult to see. "It looked just like a lightsaber," John says. "All you see is a beam of light moving around, you don't see anything else." The ocean current began pulling them toward the craggy reefs. And then the flashlight went out—they were in complete darkness. Nitanis remembers this terrifying moment. "I was praying. They [her children] had no idea what I was thinking—which of the kids I was going to be able to hold on to if the boat capsized. And so, I said, 'Put your life jackets on.' And I could see it was worrying John and Joel, but they wouldn't say anything." And then the moon started to come out, providing some light for them to navigate. They began to look at the mountain range, to find shapes and silhouettes they recognized and to use these as guides to Seitcher Bay. Nitanis recalls that moment:

We saw the mountain, the lady, her breast, her belly, her legs and her face, the mountain that we look across and see every day [at Seitcher Bay]. Once we recognized those shapes, that mountain, we knew we had to take a turn and go toward the shore. And then we made it. The kids had no idea. They were reading Archie Comics. They had no idea that I was praying to every God that I might know.

John, in particular, had a frustrating relationship with the ocean. He says, "The ocean is relentless sometimes, and I had to go and ʔuusimč (spiritual bathing) quite often and just talk, to have a conversation with the ocean. As I would ʔuusimč I would say, 'Okay, you're going to have to work on the relationship here because we need you to take care of us.'" One day in late

April 2013, after ten months of living in Seitcher Bay, the ocean finally got to John. He and his family had decided to go to an old whaling station that was situated near the bay and gather fire bricks that were going to be used to make an outdoor oven. While they were at the station the weather began to turn and it started to rain. They filled their boat quickly with bricks and headed back to Seitcher Bay.

By the time they got back to their dock the rain was pounding down hard, so they decided to leave the bricks in the boat and unload them in the morning. That night the coast was hit by a huge rainstorm with over 200 millimeters of rainfall. The next morning, John got up and went down to the dock to check on the boat. During the night the storm had caused large waves to pelt the dock, splashing over their boat and causing it to fill up with water. The boat's sump pump was not working, and because of the weight of the bricks, it had sunk. Nitanis was six months pregnant and she could not do a lot of physical activities, which then fell to their oldest daughter, Kalilah. John and Kalilah got into the water and tried to lift the boat out, spending an hour and a half in the cold ocean water before they were able to retrieve it. It was not until they got the boat turned over and back on the beach that they realized how hard they were pushing Kalilah and the responsibility they were putting on their twelve-year-old daughter. Nitanis reflects back on this event:

> We pushed the kids to a level that we would never have done any other time, to make them do those kinds of physical feats that they had to go through. That was the life [Kalilah] was leading and growing at the same time, and we were just learning and growing at the same time. But it was for our survival. Because of that experience [Kalilah] is stronger than anybody that I have known in my life. I look to her for strength. She knows the land and the waters more than anybody. And it comes from a really authentic place of being. I know that was a really good thing that we did, to give to our children, that they now know the land, they are part of that piece of territory.

After they cleaned out the boat with fresh water and fixed the broken dock where the boat had been tied, John sat down on their porch, looked at his wife, and said, "I can't do this. I can't do this anymore." John felt defeated, physically and emotionally, that he and the ocean were fighting, and that it had just beaten him up and spat him out. John says, "I was done with the ocean." Nitanis looked at her husband and said, "You can't give up." She was worried. Their boat did not work properly after the storm sank it. She was seven months pregnant. They didn't have jobs. They had no money to repair the boat and no way to get back and forth to Tofino. Nitanis thought, "What are we going to do now?" A few days later Kalilah received an invitation to perform at the "Rock the North: Stand for Mother Earth" benefit concert in Hazelton, British Columbia The money that Kalilah received was their ticket out. At the end of April 2013, ten months after moving to Seitcher Bay, Nitanis, John, and their six children packed up some of their possessions, got in their boat, and left.

"We Could've Died!": Lessons from Seitcher Bay

Nitanis says, "I tell the story, we survived. We survived Seitcher Bay. And I'd joke, we could've died. But one of my kids could have died. By all the graces of everything nobody got seriously hurt." Reflecting back on the ten months spent at Seitcher Bay, John and Nitanis try to put into perspective what they experienced. Nitanis says, "We weren't physically conditioned to do the workload that our ancestors would have done. Because we didn't have the muscle. We didn't have the core physical strength."[28] And Kalilah adds, "We didn't have people to help out." A lot of the physical duties, like chopping wood every day, fell on John, who was pushed to his physical limitations; as he states, he did not understand how much firewood they would need or the major physical duties that needed to be performed during the cold and wet winter season:

> Traditionally our ancestors had it made living as a community, because they were prepared and wintertime would be a time to find shelter, be close to your family, to celebrate. But in this particular case, we didn't have that opportunity because it was work, work, work. A lot of Indigenous people are starting to make these shifts again, back to being more Indigenous-oriented in their way of thinking and their way of doing, but for us, it was directly experiential, every single day. So we were living out that concept where a lot of people kind of were just wrestling with the shift of the worldview. There was a whole world shift for us. It was just a way different take on life.

Both Nitanis and John realized that it took an entire community to do what they attempted to do with just their young family. "We tried to do it independently. And I think it was kind of a stubborn way and it taught us valuable insights," Nitanis said. She remembers how when they first told people about what they were going to do, live off the grid, people would romanticize it, including them, thinking, as Nitanis says, "Yeah. It's going to be great." But in reflecting back she says, "It wasn't glamorous. It was cold, wet, and damp. Some of the foods we ate were sketchy. And it was lonely sometimes, especially during the really stormy days when you're basically stuck inside a 20-by-20 cabin."

Still, despite these challenges, John and Nitanis plan to go back to Seitcher Bay or another remote place in Nuu-chah-nulth homelands. But this time, there will be one major difference. They are going back with the language now that John has become fluent in Nuu-chah-nulth. This, says Nitanis, was the missing link in their life at Seitcher Bay and what they needed in order to thrive, not just survive.

> The way we needed to thrive, we needed to do it with language. There is no separation between the language and the land. Language is the key to how you interact with the land and the water. We came there like homesteaders. We brought things like colonizers brought to our lands. We were like settlers. How are we going to transform this relationship? We need to come as quu?as (Indigenous/whole person). The language was the tie, the connection that we needed.

Nitanis and John do not feel that they had failed in this experiment of living off the grid. It made them really think about the importance of language in connecting to the lands, waters, animals, and plants and doing so in a cultural way. When they returned to Port Alberni John immediately began studying and learning the language and they began incorporating language learning into their daily lives. Living in Seitcher Bay had provided them with valuable lessons, especially in how community, family, language, foods, and culture are so intimately entwined. John says the concept of "it takes a community to raise children" was so evident while they were out in Seitcher Bay, and now that they have created a strong community around language and cultural revitalization, this is going to be their strength. Or, as John says, "What we were missing before." Nitanis also feels the connection to language will be central the next time they move to Seitcher Bay and live the way of their ancestors.

> We weren't quite ready. We kind of fumbled our way onto the land. But we came back with an appreciation of the land and the ocean. Our intentions are to go back but [John is] going to bring the language, and we are going to ask the land for permission to be there, in the language. This time we are going to go in more intentionally then we had, to be more respectful and with more community support. Now we can go back and speak to the land.

John adds, "It requires us living along the land, not on it. It's a different way of communicating. Now we'll go back with a different approach, try to be more quuʔas in nature and leave less of an imprint, whereas before, we didn't think about those things. We had to go through it in order to understand it." Two months after Nitanis and John and their children left Seitcher Bay, and with Nitanis nine months pregnant, they continued their activism, got in their vehicle and drove with their six children to her Cree territory to participate in the Annual Healing Walk Gathering in Fort McMurray, Alberta, to oppose the expansion of the tar sands, the third largest oil reserves in the world, which was thirty miles away.[29] While there Nitanis went into labor, and at the stroke of midnight on July 4 she gave birth to her eighth child, Kimowanihtow, on a buffalo robe in a teepee in the middle of the gathering. In honor of her Cree heritage, his placenta was buried close to the teepee where he was born—in the lands of Nitanis's people. His umbilical cord returned to his father John's ḥaḥuułi and is now buried in Seitcher Bay along with the umbilical cords of his siblings.

Epilogue

Indigenous Health and Wellness and Living during a Time of Uncertainty

O N MARCH 6, 2020, I began self-isolation and am still in isolation as I put the final touches on this manuscript some ten months later. Many things have changed in my life as a result of the pandemic. Here in Washington State we had the first confirmed COVID-19 case in the United States on January 21, and in late February the first coronavirus-related death was announced at a long-term care facility in the Seattle suburb of Kirkland.[1] In the first week of March the University of Washington moved to online classes and remote teaching, which we continued into 2021, to remain until it is safe to hold in-person classes again. Because of the continuing health and safety uncertainties of having an in-person event, the "Living Breath of wəɫəbʔaltxʷ" Indigenous Foods symposium, which I founded in 2013 and which has been held annually in May at the UW's wəɫəbʔaltxʷ Intellectual House,[2] was cancelled.

While in isolation I have made a great effort to stay strong and healthy by taking hour-long walks each day, especially on sunny days to feel the nurturing benefits of the sun, and I have been even more conscious about eating healthy foods. The greatest challenge for me is that I am unable to travel home to my Tseshaht community because of the US and Canadian border restrictions. This was the first summer in many years when I did not process salmon and fish with my sister Gail. I was fortunate that the year before, Gail and I canned a large quantity of salmon, which has kept me well supplied with this healthy food. I usually travel back home every other month to be with my family and to immerse myself in my community and in our ceremonial and food traditions, but not with COVID. Nonetheless, I have been able to stay connected with family and friends through social media, FaceTime, and Zoom meetings (thank you, Zoom!).

My Tseshaht community, like other Indigenous communities, has felt the impact of the pandemic on our cultures. We have been unable to gather physically for Potlatches or other ceremonial gatherings. To keep our cultures strong while in social isolation, Tseshaht community members have continued to hold virtual events as a way to bring us together to share our traditional songs and provide emotional and spiritual support as we live through COVID-19.

The pandemic opened up a door to me that has actually helped me stay more connected to my culture. Because of the pandemic, the University of Victoria began holding their classes online, and one of those classes was a Nuu-chah-nulth Language class. I contacted the instructor, ƛiisƛiisaʔapt Dr. Adam Werle, to ask if I could audit the class, and he said yes. In June 2020 I began taking classes and have continued my language journey to the present. I grew up with my language but never learned to speak it fluently, and this opportunity has not only allowed me to strengthen my language skills but has kept me in virtual contact with other Nuu-chah-nulth language learners, and we have become a strong cultural support system for one another.

As mentioned in the introduction, many of our Nuu-chah-nulth communities were hit hard by the virus.[3] My nation, Tseshaht, which has a population of a little over 1,200 members with 500 living in our community, went into lockdown early in the pandemic. As of January 2021, unofficially, we had fourteen cases, with most of these members living outside our community. The low level of COVID-positive cases in our community is largely due to the great work of our frontline workers like my sister Gail, who has worked tirelessly to keep our members safe. In March Gail began putting together weekly food boxes to distribute to community members so they would stay home, lessening the spread of the virus. The food boxes were filled with nutritious foods like vegetables and fruit, and staple foods like rice, potatoes, bread, and milk, along with cleaning supplies and hand sanitizer. She also used this as an opportunity to continue to promote healthy eating and lifestyles, providing written material on how to keep safe during the pandemic and giving community members recipes for making healthy meals. During the summer Gail's garden also had more visitors, with community members getting their vegetables and fruits from the garden rather than making trips to the local town to shop for food.

Worried about their family's safety, in March Nitanis and John made the decision to leave the city of Port Alberni, where they had been living since 2013, and moved back to Seitcher Bay to live off the land once again. While there, they harvested and ate the local foods and worked on updating the cabins. It was quite a difference experience living back at Seitcher Bay now that their children were much older, Nitanis told me. "The biggest thing was that the children were not toddlers and we didn't have to worry about them. They were able to explore the bay on their own and were not as dependent on me and John."[4] They worked together in clearing the land, cultivated a garden, and built a sauna and a smokehouse.

In late August and early September the hot and dry weather produced major wildfires in eastern Washington. Heavy winds blew major smoke clouds over the west coast, with the falling ash blanketing the region and raising health concerns and warnings for people to stay inside.[5] Seitcher Bay was hit by a major smoke cloud that remained trapped in the mountains surrounding the bay. This posed a considerable health risk for Nitanis, John, and their children as they spent most of their time outdoors and also relied on fire to cook their meals and heat their cabins. In October they reluctantly moved their family back to Port Alberni. Nitanis has continued to harvest plants and has connected with other Indigenous harvesters over social media, and they have been making medicines and teas that boost immune systems and sharing these recipes on social media sites to help people stay healthy.

As this pandemic continues its devastating impact on health globally, it highlights the importance for Indigenous peoples of having access to and revitalizing our relationships to our haʔum to support and strengthen our physical, emotional, and spiritual health. This book is for everyone who has concerns about their health, and I have shown how food plays a major role in our overall physical, emotional, and dietary wellness. I hope the book has motivated you to think about the foods you eat and has encouraged you to make healthy food and life choices. The foods we eat can be our medicine; the way we live can be our medicine; the exercise we do can be our medicine; the laughter we share and positive emotional and spiritual well-being can be our medicine because ḥačatakma čawaak—everything is interconnected.

GLOSSARY

Adam Werle

This glossary lists all of the Nuu-chah-nulth and Makah words used in this book (the only Makah words are *qʷidičča?atx̌* and *six̌ʷawix̌*). The words are listed alphabetically according to their Nuu-chah-nulth or Makah spelling and are marked for their part of speech:

> n: noun, a person or thing
> tn: toponym, a place name
> a: adjective, a word that describes a noun
> v: verb, an action word
> int: interjection, a word that can stand alone as a
> complete utterance

In addition, an approximation of each word's pronunciation is given in parentheses, for the benefit of readers who do not read these alphabets. See the phonetic key at the beginning of the book for hints on the pronunciation of each letter of the Nuu-chah-nulth alphabet.

The sources for these data include many Nuu-chah-nulth elders, especially qiiqiiqiẏa Willard Gallic, tupaat Julia Lucas, and yuułnaak Simon Lucas, and scholars huuḥtakšiiḥ?ap Henry Kammler, Edward Sapir and Morris Swadesh (1939), and Denis St. Claire (1991).[1]

čišaaʔatḥ (tsi/shah/uth) (Tseshaht) n. Tseshaht person, people.

c̓uumaʕas (tsoo/muh/us) (Somass) tn. the Somass River, also the Nuu-chah-nulth name of the city of Port Alberni, "washing the earth."

čapiqƛis (chuh/pik/tlis) tn. an island in the Somass River, "island in the middle" (St. Claire, "Barkley Sound Tribal Territories," 188, 190).

c̓apac (chuh/puts) n. canoe.

c̓itaapi (chi/tah/pi) tn. Catface Mountain.

c̓iyaaqimł (chi/yah/kemlth) n. October, "fish-cutting moon."

čuu (choo) int. okay, acknowledged, goodbye.

haʔum (hah/oom) n. food.

haʔumštup (hah/oomsh/toop) n. all kinds of food.

hinkuuʔasimł (hin/koo/uh/simlth) n. September, "dog salmon moon."

hišukʔiš c̓awaak (hi/shook/ish • tsah/wahk) "Everything is one" (Central dialect).

huupačasʔatḥ (hoo/puh/chus/uth) (Hupacasath) n. Hupacasath person, people.

huyaaqimł (hoo/yah/kemlth) n. April, "flock-flying moon."

ḥačatakma c̓awaak (hah/chuh/tuk/muh • tsah/wahk) "Everything is one" (East Barkley Sound dialect).

ḥaḥuułi (hah/hoo/thli) n. chiefly territory, resources overseen by a chief.

ḥaaḥuupa (hah/hoo/puh) v. teaching in a traditional way, as grandparents teach their grandchildren.

ḥakum (hah/koom) n. queen, princess, high-ranking woman.

ḥaw̓ił (hah/wilth) n. chief.

ḥaw̓iiḥ (hah/weeh) n. chiefs.

ḥaw̓iłp̓atak ḥaw̓iiḥ (hah/wilth/puh/tuk • hah/weeh) n. traditional governance, "law of the chiefs."

ḥaay̓ištup (hah/yish/toop) n. chiton, marine mollusk.

ḥišǩʷiiʔatḥ (hesh/kwee/uth) (Hesquiaht) n. Hesquiaht person, people.

kac̓as (kuh/chus) v. barbecuing on a spit.

kac̓as miʕaat (ku/chus • mi/aht) n. barbecued sockeye salmon.

ƛaʔuukʷiʔatḥ (tlah/oo/kwi/uth) (Tla-o-qui-aht) n. Tla-o-qui-aht person, people.

ƛeekoo (tleh/koh) int. thank you, considered a formal thank-you by some elders.

mamałñi (muh/multh/ni) n. white person, settler.

masčim (mus/chim) n. villager, commoner.

maaʔak (mah/uk) n. gray whale.

miʕaat (mi/aht) n. sockeye salmon.

muwač (moo/wuch) n. deer.

ṁaayi (mah/yi) n. salmonberry shoots.

nisṁa (nis/muh) n. land, earth.

nuučaaṅuł (noo/chah/noolth) (Nuu-chah-nulth) n. mountain range, the Nuu-chah-nulth tribe, "along the mountains."

nuučaaṅułʔatḥ (noo/chah/noolth/uth) (Nuu-chah-nulth-aht) n. Nuu-chah-nulth person, people.

ṅačyuu (nuch/yoo) n. favored harvesting spot.

ṅaas (nahs) n. day, also a name of the Creator.

p̓ačiƛ (puh/chitl) v. give a Potlatch gift.

p̓uuʔi (poo/i) n. halibut.

qaałqaawi (kahlth/kah/wi) n. wild blackberries, also called trailing blackberries.

qawašimł (kuh/wuh/shimlth) n. June, "salmonberry moon."

qiłcmaʕatḥ (kelthts/mah/uth) (Kelsemaht) n. Kelsemaht person, people.

qiłcuup (kelth/tsoop) n. cow parsnip, also called wild celery, wild rhubarb, Indian rhubarb.

quuʔas (koo/us) n. person, Indian.

quuʔičiƛ (koo/i/chitl) v. growing up, becoming a person.

qʷidičča?a·tx̌ (kwi/dich/chuh/ahtkh) n. Makah person, people (Makah).

saċupimł (suh/tsoo/pimlth) n. August, "king salmon moon."

saamin (sah/min) n. salmon (from English).

saaʔaḥi (sah/ah/hey) (Tsahaheh) tn. a Tseshaht village.

siiḥṁuu (seeh/moo) n. herring roe.

six̌ʷa·wix̌ (si/khwah/wikh) n. gray whale (Makah).

tiič̓ʕaqƛ (teech/uktl) a. safe, secure, healthy, able to survive.

tuuk̓ʷasiił (too/kwuh/seelth) v. gardening.

tupaati (too/pah/ti) n. ceremonial test, privilege.

tupkaapiiḥ (toop/kah/peeh) n. Himalayan blackberries.

ƚaqwiiyak (tuk/wee/yuk) (T'aaq-wiihak) n. right to harvest, the name of a Nuu-chah-nulth fisheries organization (Julia and Simon Lucas; taaqwiihakfisheries.ca).

ƚaatṅeʔis (taht/neh/is) n. small children.

ṫuċup (too/tsoop) n. large purple sea urchin.

yaḥaak (yuh/hahk) n. salmon weir (Sapir and Swadesh, *Native Accounts of Nootka Ethnography,* 256).

ʔiisaak (ee/sahk) v. respecting it.

ʔuusimč (oo/simch) v. ritually preparing for an undertaking.

ʔuuštaqimł (oosh/tuh/kemlth) n. clan, lineage.

ʔuʔaałuk (oo/ah/thlook) v. taking care of it.

ʕaaḥuusʔatḥ (ah/hoos/uth) (Ahousaht) n. Ahousaht person, people.

NOTES

PREFACE

1   Dr. Adam Werle and Dr. Henry Kammler assisted in the Nuu-chah-nulth spelling of my family names. I was unable to find the Nuu-chah-nulth name for my grandmother, Grace Watts.

2   The Nuu-chah-nulth philosophy that everything is interconnected, commonly expressed in the phrase hišukʔiš ċawaak, is well known not only to Nuu-chah-nulth people but also to many outsiders through channels like the Nuu-chah-nulth Tribal Council (nuuchahnulth.org) and the work of Umeek Richard Atleo in his book *Tsawalk: A Nuu-chah-nulth Worldview* (Vancouver: UBC Press, 2004). The common phrase hišukʔiš ċawaak (hishuk-ish tsawalk) is in a Central Nuu-chah-nulth dialect. In my Tseshaht dialect, this phrase is written as ḥaċatakma ċawaak. yaacu-uʔisʔaqs Linsey Haggard, čiisma Della Preston, and ƛiisƛiisaʔapt Dr. Adam Werle, personal communication, January 17, 2021.

INTRODUCTION

1   Misbun is my aunt's nickname; her name is Eileen (Watts) Haggard, and her Tseshaht name is ḥeečis. The trailing blackberry, *Rubus ursinus*, is found in open forests in western North America. The berries were harvested in July and either eaten immediately or dried for later use. The tupkaapiiḥ, Himalayan blackberry, known as *Rubus discolor, R. armeniacus,* and *R. procerus,* is native to Asia and was brought to North America in the 1880s. See Kuhnlein and Turner, *Traditional Plant Foods,* 10, 166; Turner, *Earth's Blanket,* 159–66. On trailing blackberry chemistry and growth habits, see Kuhnlein and Turner, *Traditional Plant Foods,* 364; Turner, *Earth's Blanket,* 159–66.

2   Kuhnlein and Turner, *Traditional Plant Foods*, 147–77; Turner, *Earth's Blanket*, 12, 37. Nuu-chah-nulth-aht translates to the people of Nuu-chah-nulth.
3   Coulthard, *Red Skin, White Masks*, 25.
4   Tuck and Yang, "Decolonization Is Not a Metaphor," 5–6.
5   Sium, Desai, and Ritskes, "Towards the 'Tangible Unknown,'" iii.
6   Tuck and Yang, "Decolonization Is Not a Metaphor," 6; Coulthard, *Red Skin, White Masks*, 25.
7   Smith, *Decolonizing Methodologies*, 1.
8   Kovach, *Indigenous Methodologies*, 94.
9   Behrendt, "Indigenous Storytelling," 175.
10 Behrendt, "Indigenous Storytelling," 175, 177.
11 Million, "There Is a River in Me," 33.
12 The Nuu-chah-nulth philosophy that everything is interconnected is commonly expressed in the phrase hišukʔiš ćawaak (hishuk-ish tsawalk), and is well known not only to Nuu-chah-nulth people but also to many outsiders through channels like the Nuu-chah-nulth Tribal Council (nuuchahnulth.org) and the work of Umeek, Richard Atleo, in his book *Tsawalk: A Nuu-chah-nulth Worldview*. The common phrase hišukʔiš ćawaak is in a Central Nuu-chah-nulth dialect. In my Tseshaht dialect, this phrase is written as ḥaċatakma ćawaak. Personal communication, ƛiisƛiisaʔapt Dr. Adam Werle, yaacuuʔisʔaqs Linsey Haggard, and čiisma Della Preston, January 17, 2021.
13 Sium and Ritskes, "Speaking Truth to Power."
14 Million, "There Is a River in Me," 32.
15 Atleo, Umeek, *Tsawalk*, 17–18, 130; Turner et al., "Traditional Ecological Knowledge," 1279.
16 The word ńaas has many meanings in our language and can mean "day," "weather," or "Creator."
17 Atleo, Umeek, *Tsawalk*, 118.
18 Atleo, Umeek, *Tsawalk*, 10; Turner et al., "Traditional Ecological Knowledge," 1279; Raymond et al., "Ecosystem Services and Beyond," 540.
19 Happynook, "Social, Cultural and Economic Importance of Subsistence Whaling."
20 Happynook, "Social, Cultural and Economic Importance of Subsistence Whaling."
21 Turner and Turner, "'Where Our Women Used to Get the Food,'" 109.
22 Mihesuah and Hoover, *Indigenous Food Sovereignty*.
23 Shukla and Settee, *Indigenous Food Systems*.
24 Kimmerer, *Braiding Sweetgrass*.
25 Salmón, *Eating the Landscape*.
26 Krohn and Segrest, *Feeding the People, Feeding the Spirit*.
27 Marples, "Navajo Nation Faces Devastating Loss."
28 Navajo Department of Health, https://www.ndoh.navajo-nsn.gov/covid-19.

29 Goel et al., "US Food System Is Killing Americans."

30 UN Food and Agricultural Organization (FAO), Committee on World Food Security, Global Strategic Framework (GSF), http://www.fao.org/cfs/home /products/onlinegsf/1/en/.

31 For in-depth analysis and discussion on the impact of neoliberalism, globalization, capitalism, and free trade on the commodification of food production and the rise of a global market economy, see Patel, "Food Sovereignty"; Rosset, "Food Sovereignty and the Contemporary Food Crisis"; Wittman et al., "Origins and Potential of Food Sovereignty"; Trauger, "Putting Food Sovereignty in Place"; Jarosz. "Comparing Food Sovereignty"; La Via Campesina website, https://viacampesina .org/en/.

32 Anand et al., "Food Consumption and Its Impact"; Inglis and Gimlin, "Food Globalizations," 14–15.

33 Anand et al., "Food Consumption and Its Impact," 1592.

34 Holt-Giménez, "Food Security, Food Justice," 315; Anand et al., "Food Consumption and Its Impact," 1592.

35 Holt-Giménez, "Food Security, Food Justice," 315.

36 Shiva, "Food Sovereignty, Food Security," x.

37 Pollan, *Omnivore's Dilemma*, 39.

38 Corn gives cattle acidosis, causing their neutral stomachs to become acidic. It also causes them to bloat, which inflates their rumen and presses against their ribs. As a way to keep the cows healthy they are given antibiotics. Pollan, *Omnivore's Dilemma*, 66–75. See also *Food, Inc.*, an American documentary film by Robert Kenner, 2008.

39 *Food, Inc.*, examines the industrial food sector. It explores how corporate factory farming produces food that is unhealthy, environmentally destructive, and abusive to animals and the people working in these industries.

40 Kuhnlein, "Food System Sustainability," 2415.

41 Taiaiake Alfred, in Corntassel and Bryce, "Practicing Sustainable Self-Determination," 152.

42 Waziyatawin, "Paradox of Indigenous Resurgence," 72.

43 Women's Earth Alliance and Native Youth Sexual Health Network, *Violence on Our Lands*, 14.

44 Evans-Campbell, "Historical Trauma in American Indian/Native Alaska Communities," 231.

45 Evans-Campbell, "Historical Trauma in American Indian/Native Alaska Communities," 32.

46 Mohatta et al., "Historical Trauma as Public Narrative."

47 Egeland and Harrison, "Health Disparities," 17.

48 Egeland and Harrison, "Health Disparities," 18.

49 "Health Effects of Dietary Risks."

50 Pollan, *In Defense of Food*, 10.

51 Pollan, *Omnivore's Dilemma*, 81.

52 Pollan, *In Defense of Food*, 10.

53 Egeland and Harrison, "Health Disparities," 21.

54 Turner and Turner, "'Where Our Women Used to Get the Food,'" 109.

55 Egeland and Harrison, "Health Disparities," 16.

56 *Overview of Aboriginal Health in Canada*, 5.

57 *Heart Disease and Native Americans/Alaska Natives.*

58 Pollan, *In Defense of Food*, 113.

59 The *Strong Heart Study* is the largest and longest ongoing epidemiological study (currently in Phase VII) on heart disease and its risk factors among Native Americans. *Strong Heart Study, 2001 Report.*

60 *Indian Health Service Fact Sheet.*

61 *Overview of Aboriginal Health in Canada,* National Collaborating Centre for Aboriginal Health, Statistics Canada, Prince George: University of Northern British Columbia, 2013, https://www.ccnsa-nccah.ca/docs/context /FS-OverviewAbororiginalHealth-EN.pdf; Acton et al., "Trends in Diabetes Prevalence," 1487; Coté, *Spirits of Our Whaling Ancestors*, 193–97.

62 Mailer and Hale, "Decolonizing the Diet."

63 *Overview of Aboriginal Health in Canada*, 3–4.

64 Moss, *Salt, Sugar, Fat.*

65 Moss, *Salt, Sugar, Fat*, 276.

66 Blanding, *Coke Machine*, 67.

67 Story et al., "Epidemic of Obesity," 748.

68 Story et al., "Epidemic of Obesity," 751.

69 Mihesuah, "Indigenous Health Initiatives," 45.

70 Lewis, "Frybread Wars."

71 Lewis, "Frybread Wars," 429–30.

72 Pollan, *In Defense of Food*, 10.

73 Pollan, *In Defense of Food*, 141.

74 Pollan, *In Defense of Food*, 135.

75 Melanie Braker, personal communication, November 10, 2019.

76 Melanie Braker, personal communication, November 10, 2019.

CHAPTER ONE. tiičʕaqƛ

1 Green Aunty was Agnes Sam's nickname.

2 Stewart, *Cedar*; Ames and Maschner, *Peoples of the Northwest Coast.*

3 Kuhnlein and Receveur, "Dietary Change," 418.

4 Declaration of Nyéléni, Declaration of the Forum for Food Sovereignty, Sélingué, Mali, February 27, 2007, http://nyeleni.org/spip.php?article290.

5 Turner, *Earth's Blanket*, 28.

6 A chief's tupaati included rights to names, songs, dances, houses, crests, designs, harvesting sites, medicines, and knowledge. ḥawiiḥ is the plural of ḥawił and tutuupata is the plural of tupaati.

7   Quoted in Turner, *Earth's Blanket*, 170–71.

8   Nuu-chah-nulth people.

9   Kimmerer, *Braiding Sweetgrass*, 115.

10   Drucker, *Northern and Central Nootkan Tribes*, 104.

11   Drucker, *Northern and Central Nootkan Tribes*, 252; Traditional Nuu-chah-nulth Food Harvesting and Preparation, Native Studies Programme, School District No. 70 (Alberni), 30.

12   Turner, *Earth's Blanket*, 156–59.

13   Wittman et al., "Origins and Potential of Food Sovereignty," 2.

14   Wittman et al., "Origins and Potential of Food Sovereignty," 3.

15   Trauger, "Putting Food Sovereignty in Place," 4.

16   Statement by the NGO Forum to the World Food Summit, World Food Summit, November 13–17, 1996, http://www.fao.org/wfs/.

17   Declaration of Nyéléni, Declaration of the Forum for Food Sovereignty, Sélingué, Mali, February 27, 2007, http://nyeleni.org/spip.php?article290.

18   A quote from one of the Nyéléni delegates at the 2007 meeting. Trauger, "Putting Food Sovereignty in Place," 7.

19   Trauger, "Putting Food Sovereignty in Place," 4.

20   Trauger, "Putting Food Sovereignty in Place," 1.

21   Morrison, "Indigenous Food Sovereignty," 101–2.

22   Morrison, "Indigenous Food Sovereignty," 101.

23   Morrison, "Indigenous Food Sovereignty," 100–101. Also see the Indigenous Food Systems Network website, which grew out of the forums held by the WGIFS, http://www.indigenousfoodsystems.org.

24   Morrison, "Indigenous Food Sovereignty," 99.

25   United Nations Declaration on the Rights of Indigenous Peoples (2007), 8.

26   Fitzgerald and Schwartz, "Introduction," 1.

27   Last, "What Does Implementing the UNDRIP Actually Mean?"

28   Corntassel, "Toward Sustainable Self-Determination," 105–9.

29   Corntassel, "Toward Sustainable Self-Determination," 118.

30   Kimmerer, *Braiding Sweetgrass*, 115.

31   First Annual Interior of B.C. Indigenous Food Sovereignty Conference. Final Report, prepared by Dawn Morrison, September 2006, 8.

32   Kimmerer, *Braiding Sweetgrass*, 336.

33   Salmón, *Eating the Landscape*, 2.

34   Kimmerer, *Braiding Sweetgrass*, 338.

35   Grey and Patel, "Food Sovereignty as Decolonization," 437.

36   Salmón, *Eating the Landscape*, 9.

37   Salmón, *Eating the Landscape*, 9.

38   Egeland and Harrison, "Health Disparities," 21.

39   Jernigan et al., "Changing Patterns in Health Behaviors"; *Overview of Aboriginal Health in Canada*; Gracey and King, "Indigenous Health, Part 1," 70; King et al., "Indigenous Health, Part 2"; Egeland and Harrison, "Health Disparities."

40 Krohn and Segrest, *Feeding the People*, 9.

41 Krohn and Segrest, *Feeding the People*, 9.

42 Quoted in Coté, *Spirits of Our Whaling Ancestors*, 199.

43 Coté, *Spirits of Our Whaling Ancestors*, 199.

44 First Annual Interior of B.C. Indigenous Food Sovereignty Conference. Final Report, prepared by Dawn Morrison, September 2006, 11.

45 Linden, *Compass of Pleasure*; Breuning, *Meet Your Happy Chemicals*.

46 Lambden et al., "Traditional Food Attributes," 312.

47 Lambden et al., "Traditional Food Attributes," 309.

48 First Annual Interior of B.C. Indigenous Food Sovereignty Conference, Final Report, 11.

49 Salmón, *Eating the Landscape*, 8.

50 For an anthropological analysis of the Nuu-chah-nulth Potlatch, see Drucker, *Indians of the Northwest Coast*, 131–44; Drucker, *Northern and Central Nootkan Tribes*, 376–444; Drucker, *Cultures of the North Pacific Coast*, 46–47; Sapir and Swadesh, *Native Accounts of Nootka Ethnography*, 230–332. For an analysis and comparison of Northwest Coast peoples' Potlatches, see Rosman and Rubel, *Feasting with Mine Enemy*.

51 Drucker, *Northern and Central Nootkan Tribes*, 377–79; Drucker, *Indians of the Northwest Coast*; Rosman and Rubel, *Feasting with Mine Enemy*, 87–106.

52 For a Nuu-chah-nulth analysis written as a fictional account of a Potlatch, see George Clutesi's *Potlatch*.

53 Darrell Ross Sr., personal communication, August 11, 2015.

54 Darrell Ross Sr., personal communication, August 11, 2015.

55 Linda Thomas, personal communication, August 11, 2015.

56 LaDuke, "Foreword: In Praise of Seeds and Hope," xiv.

57 LaDuke, *All Our Relations*, 126–27.

58 White Earth Land Recovery Project website, https://www.welrp.org/.

59 Mihesuah and Hoover, *Indigenous Food Sovereignty*, 350.

60 Mihesuah and Hoover, *Indigenous Food Sovereignty*, 349.

61 Hoover, *From Garden Warriors to Good Seeds* blog, https://gardenwarriorsgoodseeds.com/about/; Native American Food Sovereignty Alliance (NAFSA) website, https://nativefoodalliance.org/; Slow Food Facebook page, https://www.facebook.com/Slowfoodturtleisland/.

62 Mihesuah and Hoover, *Indigenous Food Sovereignty*.

63 Krohn and Segrest, *Feeding the People*.

64 The Northwest Indian College Traditional Plants and Foods Program, https://www.nwic.edu/community/traditional-plants-and-foods/; the Muckleshoot Food Sovereignty Program, http://communityfood.wkkf.org/stories-of-innovation/muckleshoot-food-sovereignty/.

65 Dawn Morrison, personal communication, December 21, 2019.

66 First Annual Interior of B.C. Indigenous Food Sovereignty Conference, Final Report (September 2006), 5.
67 Dawn Morrison, personal communication, December 21, 2019.
68 Wild Salmon Caravan website, https://wildsalmoncaravan.ca/.
69 Morrison, Planning for Indigenous Social and Ecological Resilience. Also see Gilpin, "We Desperately Need to Be Talking about Food Sovereignty."
70 Huambachano, "Enacting Food Sovereignty"; Daigle, "Tracing the Terrain."
71 Huambachano, "Enacting Food Sovereignty," 1004.
72 Huambachano, "Enacting Food Sovereignty," 1024.
73 Haumbachano, "Enacting Food Sovereignty," 1021.
74 Haumbachano, "Enacting Food Sovereignty," 1024.
75 Daigle, "Tracing the Terrain."
76 Quoted in Daigle, "Tracing the Terrain," 306.
77 Daigle, "Tracing the Terrain," 306.
78 Daigle, "Tracing the Terrain," 309.
79 Daigle, "Tracing the Terrain," 306.
80 In my Tseshaht dialect this is written as ḥačatakma ćawaak (hachatakma tsawalk).
81 Uu-a-thluk website, https://uuathluk.ca/about/.
82 Uu-a-thluk website, https://uuathluk.ca/about/.
83 Uu-a-thluk Strategic Plan: Building on Our Successes 2018–2023, http://uuathluk.ca/wordpress/wp-content/uploads/2018/03/Uu-a-thluk-Strategic-Plan-2018-2023.pdf.
84 The phonetic spelling of gray whale is si/khwah/wikh. The Nuu-chah-nulth word for gray whale is maaʔak (mah/uk).
85 The Makah people's name for themselves is phonetically pronounced kwih-dich-chuh-aht. The name Makah came from their neighbors, the Klallam peoples, a name meaning "generous with food."
86 Coté, *Spirits of Our Whaling Ancestors*.
87 Nuu-chah-nulth hereditary chief Tom Mexsis Happynook, personal communication, June 4, 2000. Also see Happynook, "Securing Nuu-chah-nulth Food, Health and Traditional Values through the Sustainable Use of Marine Mammals," http://www.turtleisland.org/news/news-Nuuchahnulth.htm.
88 De Caterina et al., "N-3 Fatty Acids in the Treatment of Diabetic Patients," 1012–14.
89 Coté, *Spirits of Our Whaling Ancestors*.
90 Coté, *Spirits of Our Whaling Ancestors*.
91 Quoted in Ellingson, *Myth of the Noble Savage*, 367.
92 Quoted in Two Horses, "'We Know Who the Real Indians Are,'" 121.
93 Coté, "Food Sovereignty, Food Hegemony," 239.
94 From the film, *The Makah Nation: A Whaling People* (Makah Whaling Commission, 2002), quoted in Coté, *Spirits of Our Whaling Ancestors*, 154.

95 Coté, *Spirits of Our Whaling Ancestors*, 162–63.

96 Coté, *Spirits of Our Whaling Ancestors*, 255.

97 Barsh, "Food Security, Food Hegemony," 148.

98 Coté, *Spirits of Our Whaling Ancestors*, 164.

99 Gracey and King, "Indigenous Health, Part 1," 65.

100 Krohn and Segrest, *Feeding the Spirit*, 9.

101 Krohn and Segrest, *Feeding the Spirit*, 9.

102 Coté, "Whaling, Religious and Cultural Implications," 1141–42.

103 Atleo, Umeek, *Tsawalk*, 93.

104 Atleo, Umeek, *Tsawalk*, 35.

105 Kidwell, "First Foods Ceremonies and Food Symbolism," 301.

106 Kidwell, "First Foods Ceremonies and Food Symbolism," 306.

107 Kimmerer, *Braiding Sweetgrass*, 25.

108 Ambrose, "Thousands Enjoy Makah Traditional Feast."

109 Coté, *Spirits of Our Whaling Ancestors*, 202.

110 Coté, *Spirits of Our Whaling Ancestors*, 203.

111 *Anderson v. Evans*, United States Court of Appeals, Ninth Circuit, 2002, https://caselaw.findlaw.com/us-9th-circuit/1054441.html.

112 The Marine Mammal Protection Act (MMPA) bans all hunting and killing of whales "except as expressly provided for by an international treaty, convention, or agreement to which the United States is a party and which was entered into before the effective date of this subchapter or by any statute implementing any such treaty, convention or agreement." MMPA, Section 1372, (a) (2), https://www.fws.gov/international/pdf/legislation-marine-mammal -protection-act.pdf.

113 Alaska Natives have an MMPA exemption that allows them to hunt whales and marine mammals for subsistence. The US government did not issue an MMPA exemption to the Makah because of the recognized fundamental legal principle that Indian treaty rights were exempt from its provisions. The federal treaty with the Makah specifically protects the Makah's right to hunt whales. Coté, *Spirits of Our Whaling Ancestors*, 176–82. According to the court, NOAA's issuance of a gray whale quota to the Makah tribe without compliance with the MMPA violated federal law. *Anderson v. Evans* (2002), 44–45.

114 Whyte, "Food Sovereignty, Justice and Indigenous Peoples," 3.

115 Whyte, "Food Sovereignty, Justice and Indigenous Peoples," 18.

CHAPTER TWO. c̓uumaʕas

1 The Nuu-chah-nulth spelling of Tseshaht is c̓išaaʔatḥ.

2 Through elder accounts we know that the name c̓uumaʕas comes from the word ts'oma:as, which was originally used to refer to a small creek running through one of the Tseshaht village sites along the river. The meaning "cleansing" or "washing

down" refers to the autumn rains swelling the creek and washing away fish guts that were left there after the fish were cleaned. See Arima et al., *Between Ports Alberni and Renfrew*, 190. c̓uumaʕas is also the Nuu-chah-nulth name for the city of Port Alberni.

3 This information was shared by our elders with anthropologists and is recorded in Arima et al., *Between Ports Alberni and Renfrew*, 45. Also see McMillan and St. Claire, *Ts'ishaa*; McMillan and St. Claire, *Alberni Prehistory*.

4 This information comes from conversations I have had with elders throughout the years as well as from interviews that were conducted by anthropologists with community members and archaeological excavations. See Arima et al., *Between Ports Alberni and Renfrew*; McMillan and St. Claire, *Ts'ishaa*; McMillan and St. Claire, *Alberni Prehistory*.

5 Hilderbrand et al., "Role of Brown Bears (*Ursus arctos*)."

6 Whyte, "Food Sovereignty," 7.

7 For more information on First Foods ceremonies, see Clara Sue Kidwell's article, "First Foods Ceremonies and Food Symbolism."

8 See Turner, *Earth's Blanket*, 114–26; Geffen and Crawford, "First Salmon Rites"; Brown, "Fishing Rights and the First Salmon Ceremony"; Philip Drucker, *Northern and Central Nootkan Tribes*, 175–77.

9 Nuu-chah-nulth people.

10 Drucker, *Northern and Central Nootkan Tribes*, 175.

11 First Annual Interior of B.C. Indigenous Food Sovereignty Conference, Final Report, prepared by Dawn Morrison, September 2006, 8–10.

12 De Caterina et al., "N-3 Fatty Acids in the Treatment of Diabetic Patients," 1012; Breslow, "N-3 Fatty Acids and Cardiovascular Disease"; Carpenter et al., "N-3 Fatty Acids and the Metabolic Syndrome"; Connor, "N-3 Fatty Acids from Fish and Fish Oil"; Dewailly et al., "N-3 Fatty Acids and Cardiovascular Disease"; Dewailly et al., "Cardiovascular Disease Risk Factors."

13 Löfvenborg et al., "Fatty Fish Consumption"; Berbert et al., "Supplementation of Fish Oil."

14 Bentsen, "Dietary Polyunsaturated Fatty Acids."

15 Ames and Maschner, *Peoples of the Northwest Coast*, 24–29.

16 Ames and Maschner, *Peoples of the Northwest Coast*, 24–29.

17 Drucker provides an anthropological analysis of the Nuu-chah-nulth Potlatch in *Indians of the Northwest Coast*, 131–44; *Northern and Central Nootkan Tribes*, 376–444; and *Cultures of the North Pacific Coast*, 46–47. You can find Nuu-chah-nulth Potlatch stories in Sapir and Swadesh, *Native Accounts of Nootka Ethnography*.

18 Clutesi, *Potlatch*, 133–34.

19 čuu is the Nuu-chah-nulth word for "okay" or "goodbye."

20 Quoted in Turner, *Earth's Blanket*, 170.

21 Mathews and Turner, "Ocean Cultures," 189.

22 Quoted in Johnsen, "Salmon, Science and Reciprocity," 4. Parr are a juvenile life stage.

23 Mathews and Turner, "Ocean Cultures," 189; Turner, *Earth's Blanket*, 151–61.

24 Mathews and Turner, "Ocean Cultures," 189.

25 Darrell Ross Sr., personal communication, August 11, 2015. The Northwest Indigenous concept of the thirteen moons was documented by anthropologists and settlers such as Drucker, *Northern and Central Nootkan Tribes*; Sapir and Swadesh, *Native Accounts of Nootka Ethnography*; and Sproat, *Scenes and Studies of Savage Life*.

26 Johnsen, "Salmon, Science and Reciprocity."

27 Stewart, *Indian Fishing*, 99.

28 Mathews and Turner, "Ocean Cultures," 194; Johnsen, "Salmon, Science and Reciprocity," 7.

29 The mill was never maintained and shut down two years later.

30 Patricia Jimmy, personal communication, August 11, 2015.

31 The name of this island is čapiqx̣is (chuh/pik/tlis), and its history can be found in *Cultural Context of Salmon among the Tseshaht*, 70–77. This report was prepared for Tseshaht lawyer Hugh Braker by Archeo Tech Associates, a consulting firm of anthropologists, who were hired by the Tseshaht Nation in 1989 to research Tseshaht cultural connections to the Somass River for a legal case. The firm used historical records and Tseshaht oral history to create this comprehensive study.

32 Les Sam, personal communication, August 11, 2015.

33 Patricia Jimmy, personal communication, August 11, 2015.

34 Anne Robinson, personal communication, August 11, 2015.

35 Anne Robinson, personal communication, August 11, 2015.

36 Darrell Ross Sr., personal communication, August 11, 2015.

37 Johnson, "Relationship between Traditional Resource Harvesting and Traditional Knowledge," 43.

38 Johnson, "Relationship between Traditional Resource Harvesting and Traditional Knowledge," 36.

39 Patricia Jimmy, personal communication, August 11, 2015.

40 As quoted in Johnson, "Relationship between Traditional Resource Harvesting and Traditional Knowledge," 38.

41 maḥima Evelyn Georg.

42 Cathy Watts, personal communication, August 11, 2015.

43 Cathy Watts, personal communication, August 11, 2015.

44 Richard Sam Jr., personal communication, August 11, 2015.

45 Enrique Salmón, "Eating the Landscape: American Indian Stories of Food, Identity, and Resilience," YouTube, https://www.youtube.com/watch?v=iHb8QnuE788. Also see Salmón, *Eating the Landscape*.

46 Krohn and Segrest, *Feeding the People*, 33.

47 Sharon Fred, personal communication, August 11, 2015.

48 Sharon Fred, personal communication, August 11, 2015.

49 Linda Thomas, personal communication, August 11, 2015.

50 Linda Thomas, personal communication, August 11, 2015.

51 Turner, *Earth's Blanket*, 3.

52 Linda Thomas, personal communication, August 11, 2015.

53 Sharon Fred, personal communication, August 11, 2015.

54 Sharon Fred, personal communication, August 11, 2015.

55 Sharon Fred, personal communication, August 11, 2015.

56 Anne Robinson, personal communication, August 11, 2015.

57 Johnson, "Relationship between Traditional Resource Harvesting and Traditional Knowledge," 47.

58 Johnson, "Relationship between Traditional Resource Harvesting and Traditional Knowledge," 51.

59 Johnson, "Relationship between Traditional Resource Harvesting and Traditional Knowledge," 52.

60 Anne Robinson, personal communication, August 11, 2015.

61 Frank, "Traditional Foods Are Treaty Foods."

62 The Nuu-chah-nulth Research and Litigation Project, NTC website, http://www.nuuchahnulth.org/tribalcouncil/fisheries.html.

63 Dohla, "Nuu-chah-nulth Celebrate Landmark Decision."

64 Turner et al., "Global Environmental Challenges," 28.

65 Turner et al., "Global Environmental Challenges," 28.

66 Flatt and Ryan, "'Environmental Nightmare.'"

67 Weinberger, "Still Recovering."

68 Thomas, "17 Fish Farms."

69 Turner et al., "Global Environmental Challenges," 25–28.

70 Most of my relatives have nicknames, and this is the nickname my late uncle George Watts had from when he was a young boy.

71 Cheezies are a Canadian snack food made out of corn meal and powdered cheddar cheese.

CHAPTER THREE. tuukʷasiił

1 Island Health is an organization on Vancouver Island, and their Aboriginal Health Initiative Program supports community-based projects in Indigenous communities. https://www.islandhealth.ca/learn-about-health/aboriginal-health/aboriginal-health-initiative-plan-ahip, accessed December 24, 2019.

2 The United Native Nations (UNN) organization was the driving force behind this project to build a long-term care facility that prioritized Indigenous people. The UNN is an organization of Indigenous peoples and communities that support Indigenous peoples and communities in fighting for social justice. My mother Evelyn and I were members of this organization during the planning phase of this project.

Tsawaayuus opened its doors in July 1992. Tsawaayus means "rainbow" in our language. See https://rainbowgardens.ca/.

3   Gail Williams Gus, personal communication, August 12, 2017.

4   Gail Williams Gus, personal communication, July 16, 2016.

5   Sarah De Leeuw, "Intimate Colonialisms," 341.

6   Million, *Therapeutic Nations*, 2.

7   Kimmerer, *Braiding Sweetgrass*, 115.

8   tuukʷasiił means "to make a garden" or "gardening."

9   Smith, *Indigenous Peoples and Boarding Schools*, 1.

10 Adams, *Education for Extinction*, 52.

11 Davin, "Report on Industrial Schools."

12 Celia Haig-Brown was one of the first scholars in Canada to write a book about the Indian residential schools where she utilized Indigenous voices to reveal stories that had never been exposed or told outside Indigenous communities: stories about the physical, emotional, and sexual abuse and trauma that children experienced in these schools. Haig-Brown, *Resistance and Renewal*, 30.

13 Quoted in Coté, *Spirits of Our Whaling Ancestors*, 51.

14 King et al., "Indigenous Health, Part 2," 76–78.

15 Hodgson, "Rebuilding Community after Residential Schools," 94.

16 *CBC News,* "A History of Residential Schools in Canada."

17 Puxley, "Up to 6,000 Children Died."

18 Truth and Reconciliation Commission, *Honouring the Truth*, 1, http://www.trc.ca/.

19 *Indian Residential Schools*, viii.

20 De Leeuw, "Intimate Colonialisms," 343.

21 *Indian Residential Schools*, viii.

22 The Tseshaht and other Coastal Nations had winter and summer villages. Our summer villages were in the Broken Group Islands, where we lived while harvesting sea mammals and seafood. Our winter villages were where we resided most of the year, with large populations gathering together for political and social engagement and for our Potlatch ceremonies. Following colonization, the federal government enforced the reserve system, making our winter villages our principal settlements.

23 *Indian Residential Schools*, 37.

24 *Indian Residential Schools*, 35.

25 *Indian Residential Schools*, xxii.

26 AIRS shut down in August 1973.

27 *Indian Residential Schools*, 30.

28 *Indian Residential Schools*, 19.

29 *Indian Residential Schools*, 60.

30 *Indian Residential Schools*, 69.

31 *Indian Residential Schools*, 70–72.

32 *Indian Residential Schools*, 72.

33 See Adams, *Education for Extinction*; *Indian Residential Schools*; Miller, *Shingwuak's Vision*; Barman et al., *Indian Education in Canada,* vol. 1: *The Legacy*; Reyner and Eder, *American Indian Education*; and Million, "Felt Theory."

34 TRC, *Honouring the Truth*, 86.

35 TRC, *Honouring the Truth*, 88.

36 TRC, *Honouring the Truth*, 91.

37 Mosby, "Administering Colonial Science."

38 This study, "Medical Survey of Nutrition among the Northern Manitoba Indians," was conducted by Moore, Kruse, Tisdall, and Corrigan, and was published in the March 1946 volume of the *Canadian Medical Association Journal*. Mosby, "Administering Colonial Science," 146.

39 Mosby, "Administering Colonial Science," 146.

40 Mosby, "Administering Colonial Science," 161.

41 Mosby, "Administering Colonial Science," 161–62.

42 Mosby, "Administering Colonial Science," 165.

43 Mosby, "Administering Colonial Science," 162.

44 Quoted in Morrow, "Canada Must Apologize."

45 Quoted in Morrow, "Canada Must Apologize."

46 Morrow, "Canada Must Apologize."

47 Mosby, "Administering Colonial Science," 148.

48 *Indian Residential Schools*, 1.

49 Million, "Felt Theory," 73.

50 Mitchell et al., "Colonial Trauma," 79–80.

51 Jernigan et al., "Changing Patterns in Health Behaviors"; *An Overview of Aboriginal Health in Canada*; Gracey and King, "Indigenous Health, Part 1," 70; King et al., "Indigenous Health, Part 2," 79.

52 Mosby and Galloway, "'Hunger Was Never Absent.'"

53 See Adams, *Education for Extinction*; and see *Indian Residential Schools*; Miller, *Shingwuak's Vision*; Barman et al., *Indian Education in Canada*; Reyner and Eder, *American Indian Education*; and Million, "Felt Theory."

54 TRC, *Honouring the Truth*.

55 Million, *Therapeutic Nations*, 6.

56 Quoted in Mosby, "Administering Colonial Science," 170.

57 Crawford, "Guardian Spirit Complex," 356.

58 Kimmerer, *Braiding Sweetgrass*, 17.

59 Kimmerer, *Braiding Sweetgrass*, 336.

60 Gail Williams Gus, personal communication, August 10, 2015.

61 Gail Williams Gus, personal communication, August 12, 2017.

62 Gail Williams Gus, personal communication, December 24, 2019.

63 Gail Williams Gus, personal communication, July 2016.

64 The three sisters, beans, corn, and squash, are important agricultural crops for many Indigenous peoples in North America and are central to their cultures and

foodways. The corn stalks provide support for the bean vines, the beans provide nitrogen for the corn, and the large leaves of the squash plant provide shade and help prevent weed growth.

65 Gail Williams Gus, personal communication, July 16, 2016.

66 Gail Williams Gus, personal communication, July 16, 2016.

67 The Haahuupayuk school was originally called Ha-Ho-Payuk and was built in 1976 to provide culturally relevant education to Nuu-chah-nulth children. The school is open to other Indigenous and non-Indigenous children. An agreement was made with Nuu-chah-nulth ḥaw̓iiḥ (chiefs/leaders) that since the school was erected on Tseshaht land, the curriculum would be based in Tseshaht culture and traditions. Morrow, "40th Year Shaping Up."

68 The word t̓aat̓ne?is means "children" in our language.

69 Gail Williams Gus, personal communication, December 24, 2019.

70 Gail Williams Gus, personal communication, December 24, 2019.

71 Plummer, "Tseshaht Community Garden Adds 30 Fruit Trees."

72 Gail Williams Gus, personal communication, December 24, 2019.

73 Shaunee Thomas, personal communication, January 22, 2020.

74 Laura Johnson, personal communication, January 6, 2020.

75 Laura Johnson, personal communication, January 6, 2020.

76 Kimmerer, *Braiding Sweetgrass*, 136.

77 Titian, "Reclaiming Lost Souls."

78 Gail Williams Gus, personal communication, December 24, 2019.

79 Gail Williams Gus, personal communication, August 12, 2017.

80 Gail Williams Gus, personal communication, December 24, 2019.

CHAPTER FOUR. quu?ičiⱡ

1 kamâmakskwew is Nitanis's Cree name, and it means Butterfly Woman. waakiituusiis is Nitanis's Nuu-chah-nulth name, and it refers to when the sun and moon are visible in the sky at the same time.

2 This is John's Nuu-chah-nulth name and means "taking care of the day."

3 The word quu?ičiⱡ literally means to grow up or become a whole person. It is pronounced koo-ichitl.

4 We use the word quu?as to refer to Indigenous people. It is phonetically pronounced koo-us.

5 John Rampanen, personal communication, December 23, 2019.

6 wəɬəb?altxʷ is a Lushootseed word that translates to English as "Intellectual House."

7 You can find Kalilah's music on YouTube and on her Facebook page under her name, Kalilah Rampanen.

8 The Native Youth Movement mission is to defend Indigenous peoples and territories through education, agitation, and direct action. Indigenous Resistance Archive, January 27, 2019, https://indigenousarchive.wordpress. com/2019/01/27/what-is-the-native-youth-movement/.

9   Nitanis Desjarlais, personal communication, August 12, 2015.

10 Formerly known as Malaspina University-College, the school became VIU in 2008.

11 The West Coast Warrior Society dissolved in 2005 after numerous raids by Canada's Royal Canadian Mounted Police (RCMP) forces, and members began fearing for the safety of their families. "Warrior Society Dissolves," *Globe and Mail*, August 4, 2005, https://www.theglobeandmail.com/news/national/warrior-society-dissolves/article18242623/.

12 The VICCIFN is a collective of members who foster and support the revitalization of First Nations foodways. https://indigenousfoods.docu.li/#:~:text=The%20Vancouver%20Island%20%26%20Coastal%20Communities,Nations%20cultural%20teachings%20and%20practices.

13 Nitanis Desjarlais, personal communication, August 12, 2015.

14 Nitanis Desjarlais, personal communication, December 23, 2019.

15 Nitanis Desjarlais, personal communication, August 12, 2015; following quotes are also from this date. Oolichan is a small, oily fish in the smelt family.

16 John told me that the Seitcher family holds a hereditary chieftainship in Tla-o-qui-aht. Around the time of the Ahousaht war (early to mid-1800s) the Seitchers moved to Ahousaht territory to evade a series of deaths aimed at overtaking the hereditary position. Seitcher Bay was the area provided by tayii ḥaẃił (head chief) Maquinna in Ahousaht. The Seitchers also received a seat within Maquinna's house. Since then many family members have returned to Tla-o-qui-aht territory and the hereditary chieftainship was re-established. Some family members, such as John's, have maintained their Ahousaht affiliation. Personal communication, John Rampanen, December 23, 2019; following quotes are from the December interview unless otherwise indicated.

17 Nitanis Desjarlais, personal communication, August 12, 2015.

18 John Rampanen, personal communication, December 23, 2019; following quotes are from the December interview unless otherwise indicated.

19 Nitanis Desjarlais, personal communication, December 23, 2019.

20 John Rampanen, personal communication, August 12, 2015; following quotes are from the August interview unless otherwise indicated.

21 Kalilah Rampanen, personal communication, December 23, 2019.

22 See the Oak and Orca website, https://oakandorca.ca/.

23 Nitanis Desjarlais and John Rampanen, personal communication, December 23, 2019.

24 Kalilah has continued her music path and has recorded many songs, which can be found on YouTube.

25 Nitanis Desjarlais, personal communication, December 23, 2019.

26 Nitanis Desjarlais and John Rampanen, personal communication, December 23, 2019; following quotes from them and Kalilah are from the December interview unless otherwise indicated.

27 Nitanis Desjarlais, personal communication, December 23, 2019; following quotes are from the December interview unless otherwise indicated.

28 Nitanis Desjarlais, personal communication, December 23, 2019; following quotes
    are from the December interview unless otherwise indicated.
29 The tar sands are a mixture of sand, clay, and a heavy crude oil or tarry sub-
    stance called bitumen and lie beneath 10.6 million acres (4.3 million hectares)
    in northern Alberta; they constitute the second largest source of oil in the world.
    The tar sands have been described as one of the worst environmentally destructive
    extractive projects in the world, and mining them has created serious health issues
    for the Indigenous peoples living in this area, with high rates of cancers. Nitanis's
    people, the Fort McMurray First Nation, is one of these communities impacted by
    the tar sands. The ecosystem, including the animals and plants on which these
    Indigenous peoples subsist, have been seriously impacted by the elevated levels of
    heavy metals and carcinogens coming from the tar sands. https://www.ienearth
    .org/what-we-do/tar-sands/.

EPILOGUE

1   McNerthney, "Coronavirus in Washington State."
2   The wəłəbʔaltxʷ Intellectual House is a project I chaired, and our goal was to
    build a coastal longhouse-style building on our campus to serve as a visible symbol
    honoring the region's Indigenous peoples while exemplifying the spirit of sharing,
    cooperation, and commitment to Indigenous knowledge. On March 12, 2015, we
    opened the doors to the wəłəbʔaltxʷ with completion of phase one of the project.
3   Quinn, "Nuu-chah-nulth Nations on Vancouver Island Hit Hard by COVID-19."
4   Nitanis Desjarlais, personal communication, January 25, 2021.
5   Austen, "Wildfire Smoke Chokes Canada's Western Skies."

GLOSSARY

1   Sapir and Swadesh, *Nootka Texts*; St. Claire, "Barkley Sound Tribal Territories."

BIBLIOGRAPHY

Acton, Kelly J., Nilka Rios Burrows, Kelly Moore, Linda Querec, Linda S. Geiss, and Michael M. Engelgau. "Trends in Diabetes Prevalence among American Indian and Alaska Native Children, Adolescents, and Young Adults." *American Journal of Public Health* 92, no. 9 (September 2002): 1485–90.

Adams, David W. *Education for Extinction: American Indians and the Boarding School Experience, 1875–1928.* Lawrence: University of Kansas Press, 1995.

Aday, Serpil, and Mehmet Seckin Aday. "Impact of COVID-19 on the Food Supply Chain." *Food Quality and Safety* 4, no. 4 (December 2020): 167–80.

Ambrose, Denise. "Thousands Enjoy Makah Traditional Feast." *Ha-Shilth-Sa*, June 3, 1999, 1, 10.

Ames, Kenneth M., and Herbert D. G. Maschner. *Peoples of the Northwest Coast: Their Archaeology and Prehistory.* New York: Thames & Hudson, 1999.

Anand, Sonia S., Corinna Hawkes, Russell J. de Souza, Andrew Mente, Mahshid Dehghan, Rachel Nugent, Michael A. Zulyniak, Tony Weis, Adam M. Bernstein, Ronald M. Krauss, Daan Kromhout, David J. A. Jenkins, Vasanti Malik, Miguel A. Martinez-Gonzalez, Dariush Mozaffarian, Salim Yusuf, Walter C. Willet, and Barry M. Popkin. "Food Consumption and Its Impact on Cardiovascular Disease: Importance of Solutions Focused on the Globalized Food System—A Report from the Workshop Convened by the World Heart Federation." *Journal of American College of Cardiology* 66, no. 14 (2015): 1590–1614.

Anderson v. Evans. United States Court of Appeals, Ninth Circuit, 2002. https://caselaw .findlaw.com/us-9th-circuit/1054441.html.

Arima, E. Y., Denis St. Claire, Louise Clamhouse, Joshua Edgar, Charles Jones, and John Thomas. *Between Ports Alberni and Renfrew: Notes on West Coast Peoples.* Mercury Series. Hull, QC: Canadian Museum of Civilization, 1991.

Atleo, E. Richard, Umeek. *Tsawalk: A Nuu-chah-nulth Worldview.* Vancouver: UBC Press, 2004.

Austen, Ian. "Wildfire Smoke Chokes Canada's Western Skies." *New York Times,* September 14, 2020. https://www.nytimes.com/2020/09/14/world/americas/wildfires-canada-smoke.html.

Barman, Jean, Yvonne Hébert, and Don McCaskill. *Indian Education in Canada.* Vol. 1: *The Legacy.* Vancouver: UBC Press, 1986.

Barsh, Russel Lawrence. "Food Security, Food Hegemony, and Charismatic Animals." In *Toward a Sustainable Whaling Regime,* edited by Robert L. Friedman, 171–86. Seattle: University of Washington Press, 2001.

Behrendt, Larissa. "Indigenous Storytelling: Decolonizing Institutions and Assertive Self-Determination: Implications for Legal Practice." In *Decolonizing Research: Indigenous Storywork as Methodology,* edited by Jo-ann Archibald Q'um Xiien, Jenny Bol Jun Lee-Morgan, and Jason De Santalo, 175–86. London: Zed Books, 2019.

Bentsen, Håvard. "Dietary Polyunsaturated Fatty Acids, Brain Function and Mental Health." *Microbial Ecology in Health and Disease* 28 (2017). Open access journal, DOI: 10.1080/16512235.2017.1281916.

Berbert, Alfredo Alair, Cacilda Rosa Mitiko Kondo, Cecília Lisete Almendra, Tiemi Matsuo, and Isaias Dichi. "Supplementation of Fish Oil and Olive Oil in Patients with Rheumatoid Arthritis." *Nutrition* 21 (2005): 131–36.

Blanding, Michael. *The Coke Machine: The Dirty Truth behind the World's Favorite Soft Drink.* New York: Penguin Books, 2011.

Braker, Melanie. Personal communication, November 10, 2019.

Breslow, Jan L. "N-3 Fatty Acids and Cardiovascular Disease." *American Journal of Clinical Nutrition* 83 (2006): 1477–82.

Breuning, Loretta G. *Meet Your Happy Chemicals.* Inner Mammal Institute, 2012. www.InnerMammalInstitute.org.

Brown, Jovanna. "Fishing Rights and the First Salmon Ceremony." In *American Indian Religious Traditions,* edited by Suzanne J. Crawford and Dennis F. Kelly, 320–24. Santa Barbara: ABC/CLIO, 2005.

Carpentier, Yvon A., Laurence Portois, and Willy J. Malaisse. "N-3 Fatty Acids and the Metabolic Syndrome." *American Journal of Clinical Nutrition* 83 (2006): 1499–1504.

CBC News. "A History of Residential Schools in Canada." March 16, 2008. Updated on March 21, 2016. https://www.cbc.ca/news/canada/a-history-of-residential-schools-in-canada-1.702280.

Chino, Michelle, Darlene R. Haff, and Carolee Dodge Francis. "Patterns of Commodity Food Use among American Indians." *Environmental and Occupational Health* 7, no. 2 (2009): 279–89. https://digitalscholarship.unlv.edu/cgi/viewcontent.cgi?article=1050&context=env_occ_health_fac_articles.

Clutesi, George. *Potlatch.* Sidney, BC: Gray Publishing, 1969.

Connor, William E. "N-3 Fatty Acids from Fish and Fish Oil: Panacea or Nostrum?" *American Journal of Clinical Nutrition* 74 (2001): 415–16.

Corntassel, Jeff. "Toward Sustainable Self-Determination: Rethinking the Contemporary Indigenous-Rights Discourse." *Alternatives* 33 (2008): 105–32.

Corntassel, Jeff, and Cheryl Bryce. "Practicing Sustainable Self-Determination." *Brown Journal of World Affairs* 28, no. 11 (Spring–Summer 2012): 151–62.

Coté, Charlotte. "Food Sovereignty, Food Hegemony, and the Revitalization of Indigenous Whaling Practices." In *The World of the Indigenous Americas*, edited by Robert Allen Warrior, 239–62. New York: Routledge, 2015.

———. *"hishuk'ish tsawalk*—Everything Is One: Revitalizing Place-Based Indigenous Food Systems through the Enactment of Food Sovereignty." Special issue, Global Indigeneities and the Environment, *Journal of Agriculture, Food Systems, and Community Development* 9, no. A (2019): 37–48.

———. "'Indigenizing' Food Sovereignty: Revitalizing Indigenous Food Practices and Ecological Knowledges in Canada and the United States." *Humanities* 5, no. 3 (Spring 2016): 1–14. https://www.mdpi.com/2076-0787/5/3/57/htm.

———. *Spirits of Our Whaling Ancestors: Revitalizing Makah and Nuu-chah-nulth Traditions.* Seattle: University of Washington Press, 2010.

———. "Whaling, Religious and Cultural Implications." In *American Indian Religious Traditions*, edited by Suzanne J. Crawford and Dennis F. Kelly, 1141–53. Santa Barbara: ABC-CLIO, 2005.

Coulthard, Glen. *Red Skin, White Masks: Rejecting the Colonial Politics of Recognition.* Minneapolis: University of Minnesota Press, 2014.

Crawford, Suzanne J. "The Guardian Spirit Complex." In *American Indian Religious Traditions*, edited by Suzanne J. Crawford and Dennis F. Kelly, 355–60. Santa Barbara: ABC-CLIO, 2005.

Cultural Context of Salmon among the Tseshaht: Native Ownership and Utilization of the Somass River, Port Alberni, B.C. Report prepared for Hugh Braker, Barrister and Solicitor, by Archeo Tech Associates. Victoria, BC, June, 1989.

Daigle, Michelle. "Tracing the Terrain of Indigenous Food Sovereignties." *Journal of Peasant Studies* 46, no. 2 (2019): 297–315.

Davin, Nicholas Flood. "Report on Industrial Schools for Indians and Half-Breeds." Canada. Annual Report, 1880, Department of the Interior, March 14, 1879.

De Caterina, Raffaele, Alessandra Bertolotto, Rosalinda Madonna, and Erik Berg Schmidt. "N-3 Fatty Acids in the Treatment of Diabetic Patients." *Diabetes Care* 30, no. 4 (April 2007): 1012–26.

Declaration of Nyéléni, Declaration of the Forum for Food Sovereignty, Sélingué, Mali, February 27, 2007. http://nyeleni.org/spip.php?article290.

De Leeuw, Sarah. "Intimate Colonialisms: The Material and Experienced Places of British Columbia's Residential Schools." *Canadian Geographer* 51, no. 3 (2007): 339–59.

Desjarlais, kamâmakskwew, waakiituusiis Nitanis. Personal communication, August 12, 2015; December 23, 2019; January 23 and 31, 2021.

Dewailly, Eric, Carole Blanchet, Suzanne Gingras, Simone Lemieux, and Bruce John Holub. "Cardiovascular Disease Risk Factors and N-3 Fatty Acid Status in the Adult

Population of James Bay Cree." *American Journal of Clinical Nutrition* 76, no. 1 (July 2002): 85–92.

Dewailly, Eric, Carole Blanchet, Simone Lemieux, Louise Sauvé, Suzanne Gingras, Pierre Ayotte, and Bruce John Holub. "N-3 Fatty Acids and Cardiovascular Disease Risk Factors among the Inuit of Nunavik." *American Journal of Clinical Nutrition* 74 (2001): 464–73.

Dohla, Lloyd. "Nuu-chah-nulth Celebrate Landmark Decision." *First Nations Drum,* November 27, 2009. http://www.firstnationsdrum.com/2009/11/nuu-chah-nulth -celebrate-landmark-fisheries-decision/.

Drucker, Philip. *Cultures of the North Pacific Coast.* San Francisco: Chandler Publishing Company, 1965.

———. *Indians of the Northwest Coast.* Ottawa: Carleton University Press, 1955.

———. *The Northern and Central Nootkan Tribes.* Bulletin 144, Bureau of American Ethnology. Washington, DC: Smithsonian Institution, 1951.

Egeland, Grace M., and Gail G. Harrison. "Health Disparities: Promoting Indigenous Peoples' Health through Traditional Food Systems and Self-Determination." In *Indigenous Peoples' Food Systems & Well-Being: Interventions & Policies for Healthy Communities,* edited by V. Harriet Kuhnlein, Bill Erasmus, Dina Spigelski, and Barbara Burlingame, 9–22. Rome: Food and Agriculture Organization of the United Nations & Centre for Indigenous Peoples' Nutrition and Environment, 2013.

Ellingson, Ter. *The Myth of the Noble Savage.* Berkeley: University of California Press, 2001.

Evans-Campbell, Teresa. "Historical Trauma in American Indian/Native Alaska Communities: A Multilevel Framework for Exploring Impacts on Individuals, Families, and Communities." *Journal of Interpersonal Violence* 23, no. 3 (March 2008): 316–38.

First Annual Interior of B.C. Indigenous Food Sovereignty Conference. Final Report, prepared by Dawn Morrison, September 2006.

Fitzgerald, Oonagh, and Risa Schwartz. "Introduction." In *UNDRIP Implementation Braiding International, Domestic and Indigenous Laws, Special Report.* Waterloo, ON: Centre for International Governance Innovation, 2017.

Flatt, Courtney, and John Ryan. "'Environmental Nightmare' after Thousands of Atlantic Salmon Escape Fish Farm." National Public Radio podcast, *Salt: What's on Your Plate?* August 24, 2017. https://www.npr.org/sections/thesalt/2017/08/24 /545619525/environmental-nightmare-after-thousands-of-atlantic-salmon-escape -fish-farm.

Frank, Billy, Jr. "Traditional Foods Are Treaty Foods." Northwest Treaty Tribes. https://nwtreatytribes.org/traditional-foods-are-treaty-foods/. Accessed August 24, 2019.

Fred, Sharon. Personal communication, August 11, 2015.

Geffen, Joel, and Suzanne Crawford. "First Salmon Rites." In *American Indian Religious Traditions,* 311–19. Santa Barbara: ABC/CLIO, 2005.

Gilpin, Emily. "We Desperately Need to Be Talking about Food Sovereignty." *National Observer*, June 9, 2020. https://www.nationalobserver.com/2020/06/09/features /we-desperately-need-be-talking-about-food-sovereignty.

Goel, Akash, Michel Nischan, Bill Frist, and Tom Colicchio. "The US Food System Is Killing Americans." CNN, August 7, 2020. https://www.cnn.com/2020/08/02 /opinions/us-nutrition-insecurity-snap-goel-nischan-frist-coliccio/.

Gracey, Michael, and Malcolm King. "Indigenous Health, Part 1: Determinants and Disease Patterns." *Lancet* 374, no. 9683 (2009): 65–75.

Grey, Sam, and Raj Patel. "Food Sovereignty as Decolonization: Some Contributions from Indigenous Movements to Food Systems and Development Politics." *Agriculture & Human Values* 32, no. 1 (2015):431–44. http://works.bepress.com /samgrey/19/. Accessed October 10, 2015.

Gus, Gail Williams. Personal communication, August 10, 2015; July 16, 2016; August 12, 2017; December 24, 2019; January 31, 2021.

Haggard, yaacuu?is?aqs Linsey. Personal communication, January 17, 2021.

Haig-Brown, Celia. *Resistance and Renewal: Surviving the Indian Residential School.* Vancouver: Arsenal Pulp Press, 1988.

Happynook, Tom Mexsis. "Securing Nuu-chah-nulth Food, Health and Traditional Values through the Sustainable Use of Marine Mammals." Brentwood Bay, BC: World Council of Whalers, 2001. http://www.turtleisland.org/news/news -Nuuchahnulth.htm.

———. "The Social, Cultural and Economic Importance of Subsistence Whaling." http://oregonstate.edu/dept/IIFET/2000/abstracts/happynook.html.

"Health Effects of Dietary Risks in 195 Countries, 1990–2017: A Systematic Analysis for the Global Burden of Disease Study 2017." *Lancet* 393 (2019): 1958–72.

Healy, Jack. "Tribal Elders Are Dying from the Pandemic, Causing a Cultural Crisis for American Indians." *New York Times*, January 12, 2021. https://www.nytimes .com/2021/01/12/us/tribal-elders-native-americans-coronavirus.html

Heart Disease and Native Americans/Alaska Natives. US Department of Health and Human Services, Office of Minority Health. https://minorityhealth.hhs.gov/omh /browse.aspx?lvl = 4&lvlid = 34. Accessed January 5, 2020.

Hilderbrand, Grant V., Thomas A. Hanley, Charles T. Robbins, and Charles C. Schwartz. "Role of Brown Bears (*Ursus arctos*) in the Flow of Marine Nitrogen into a Terrestrial Ecosystem." *Oecologia* 121 (1999): 546–50.

Hodgson, Maggie. "Rebuilding Community after Residential Schools." *Nation to Nation: Aboriginal Sovereignty and the Future of Canada,* 2nd ed., edited by John Bird, Lorraine Land, and Murray Macadam, 92–108. Toronto: Public Justice Resource Centre, 2002.

Holt-Giménez, Eric. "Food Security, Food Justice, or Food Sovereignty: Crisis, Food Movements, and Regime Change." In *Cultivating Food Justice: Race, Class, and Sustainability,* edited by Alison Hope Alkon and Julian Agyeman, 309–30. Cambridge: MIT Press, 2011.

Hoover, Elizabeth. *From Garden Warriors to Good Seeds* blog. https://gardenwarriors-goodseeds.com/about/. Accessed May 2, 2019.

Hopping, B. N., E. Erber, E. Mead, T. Sheehy, C. Roache, and S. Sharma. "Socioeconomic Indicators and Frequency of Traditional Food, Junk Food, and Fruit and Vegetable Consumption amongst Inuit Adults in the Canadian Arctic." *Journal of Human Nutrition and Diet* 23, no. 1 (2010): 51–58.

Huambachano, Mariaelena. "Enacting Food Sovereignty in Aotearoa New Zealand and Peru: Revitalizing Indigenous Knowledge, Food Practices and Ecological Philosophies." *Agroecology and Sustainable Food Systems* 42, no. 9 (2018): 1003–28.

Indian Health Service Fact Sheet. U.S. Depart of Indian Health Services. https://www.ihs.gov/newsroom/index.cfm/factsheets/disparities/. Accessed January 5, 2020.

Indian Residential Schools: The Nuu-chah-nulth Experience. Nuu-chah-nulth Tribal Council Indian Residential School Study, 1992–94. Port Alberni: Nuu-chah-nulth Tribal Council, 1996.

Indigenous Food Systems Network. http://www.indigenousfoodsystems.org/. Accessed September 10, 2015.

Indigenous Resistance Archive. The Native Youth Movement. January 27, 2019. https://indigenousarchive.wordpress.com/2019/01/27/what-is-the-native-youth-movement/.

Inglis, David, and Debra Gimlin. "Food Globalizations: Ironies and Ambivalences of Food, Cuisine and Globality." In *The Globalization of Food*, edited by David Inglis and Debra Gimlin, 3–44. Oxford, UK: Berg Publishers, 2009.

Jarosz, Lucy. "Comparing Food Sovereignty, Food Security Discourses." *Dialogues in Human Geography* 4 (2014): 168–81.

Jernigan, Valerie Blue Bird, Bonnie Duran, David Ahn, and Marilyn Winkleby. "Changing Patterns in Health Behaviors and Risk Factors Related to Cardiovascular Disease among Indians and Alaska Natives." *American Journal of Public Health* 100, no. 4 (April 2010): 677–83.

Jimmy, Patricia. Personal communication, August 11, 2015.

Johnsen, Bruce. "Salmon, Science and Reciprocity on the Northwest Coast." *Ecology & Society* 14, no. 2 (December 2009). http://www.ecologyandsociety.org/vol14/iss2/art43/.

Johnson, Janice (Tliniihak Wemptis). "Relationship between Traditional Resource Harvesting and Traditional Knowledge Transfer of Ts'ishaa7ath." Master's thesis, Vancouver Island University, Nanaimo, British Columbia, February 2014.

Johnson, Laura. Personal communication, January 22, 2020.

Kenner, Robert, dir. *Food, Inc.* 2008. Documentary film.

Kidwell, Clara Sue. "First Foods Ceremonies and Food Symbolism." In *American Indian Religious Traditions*, edited by Suzanne J. Crawford and Dennis F. Kelly, 301–7. Santa Barbara: ABC-CLIO, 2005.

Kimmerer, Robin Wall. *Braiding Sweetgrass: Indigenous Wisdom, Scientific Knowledge, and the Teachings of Plants*. Minneapolis: Milkweed Editions, 2013.

King, Malcolm, Alexandra Smith, and Michael Gracey. "Indigenous Health, Part 2: The Underlying Causes of the Health Gap." *Lancet* 374, no. 9683 (2009): 76–85.

Kovach, Margaret. *Indigenous Methodologies: Characteristics, Conversations, and Contexts.* Toronto: University of Toronto Press, 2009.

Krohn, Elise, and Valerie Segrest. *Feeding the People, Feeding the Spirit: Revitalizing Northwest Coastal Indian Food Culture.* Bellingham, WA: Northwest Indian College, 2010.

Kuhnlein, Harriet V. "Food System Sustainability for Health and Well-Being of Indigenous Peoples." *Public Health Nutrition* 18, no. 13 (December 2014): 2415–24.

Kuhnlein, Harriet V., and Olivier Receveur. "Dietary Change and Traditional Food Systems of Indigenous Peoples." *Annual Review of Nutrition* 16 (1996): 417–42. www.annualreviews.org/aronline.

Kuhnlein, Harriett V., and Nancy J. Turner. *Traditional Plant Foods of Canadian Indigenous Peoples: Nutrition, Botany, and Use.* Amsterdam: Gordon and Breach –Overseas Publishers Association, 1991. http://www.hscdsb.on.ca/wp-content /uploads/2017/03/plantfoods_indigenous.pdf.

LaDuke, Winona. *All Our Relations: Native Struggles for Land and Life.* Cambridge, MA: South End Press, 1999.

———. "Foreword: In Praise of Seeds and Hope." In *Indigenous Food Sovereignty in the United States: Restoring Cultural Knowledge, Protecting Environments, and Regaining Health,* by Devon A. Mihesuah and Elizabeth Hoover, xiii–xvi. Norman: University of Oklahoma Press, 2019.

Lambden, Jill, Olivier Receveur, and Harriet V. Kuhnlein. "Traditional Food Attributes Must Be Included in Studies of Food Security in the Canadian Arctic." *International Journal of Circumpolar Health* 66, no. 4 (2007): 308–19.

Last, John. "What Does Implementing the UNDRIP Actually Mean?" *CBC News,* November 2, 2019. https://www.cbc.ca/news/canada/north/implementing -undrip-bc-nwt-1.5344825.

La Via Campesina website. https://viacampesina.org/en/. Accessed February 15, 2016.

Lewis, Courtney. "Frybread Wars: Biopolitics and the Consequences of Selective United States Healthcare Practices for American Indians." *Food, Culture & Society* 21, no. 4 (2018): 427–48. DOI: 10.1080/15528014.2018.1480644.

Linden, David J. *The Compass of Pleasure: How Our Brains Make Fatty Foods, Orgasm, Exercise, Marijuana, Generosity, Vodka, Learning, and Gambling Feel So Good.* New York: Penguin Books, 2012.

Löfvenborg, J. E., T. Andersson, S. Carlsson, M. Dorkhan, L. Groop, M. Martinell, T. Tuomi, and A. Wolk. "Fatty Fish Consumption and Risk of Latent Autoimmune Diabetes in Adults." *Nutrition & Diabetes* (2014): 1–6.

Mailer, Gideon, and Nicola Hale. "Decolonizing the Diet: Synthesizing Native-American History, Immunology, and Nutritional Science." *Journal of Evolution and Health* 1, no. 1, article 7 (2013): 1–41. https://escholarship.org/content/qt83n957nb /qt83n957nb.pdf?t=q3sazi.

The Makah Nation: A Whaling People (film). Makah Whaling Commission, 2002.

Marine Mammal Protection Act (MMPA). https://www.fws.gov/international/pdf /legislation-marine-mammal-protection-act.pdf. Accessed March 11, 2019.

Marples, Megan. "Navajo Nation Faces Devastating Loss from Covid-19 Pandemic." CNN, November 24, 2020. https://www.cnn.com/2020/11/24/health/navajo -nation-coronavirus-losses-wellness/index.html.

Mathews, Darcy L., and Nancy J. Turner. "Ocean Cultures: Northwest Coast Ecosystems and Indigenous Management Systems." In *Conservation for the Anthropocene Ocean: Interdisciplinary Science in Support of Nature and People,* edited by Phillip S. Levin and Melissa R. Poe, 169–99. London: Academic Press, 2017.

McMillan, Alan D., and Denis E. St. Claire. *Alberni Prehistory: Archeological and Ethnographic Investigations on Western Vancouver Island.* Penticton, BC: Theytus Books, 1982.

———. *Ts'ishaa: Archaeology and Ethnography of a Nuu-chah-nulth Origin Site in Barkley Sound.* Burnaby, BC: Simon Fraser University Archaeology Press, 2005.

McNerthney, Casey. "Coronavirus in Washington State: A Timeline of the Outbreak through March 2020." KIRO 7 News, April 3, 2020. https://www.kiro7.com/news /local/coronavirus-washington-state-timeline-outbreak/IM65JK66N5BYTIAPZ 3FUZSKMUE/.

Mihesuah, Devon. "Indigenous Health Initiatives, Frybread, and the Marketing of Non-traditional 'Traditional' American Indian Foods." *NAIS* 3, no. 2 (2016): 45–69.

Mihesuah, Devon A., and Elizabeth Hoover, eds. *Indigenous Food Sovereignty in the United States: Restoring Cultural Knowledge, Protecting Environments, and Regaining Health.* Norman: University of Oklahoma Press, 2019.

Miller, J. R. *Shingwuak's Vision: A History of Native Residential Schools.* Toronto: University of Toronto Press, 1996.

Million, Dian. "Felt Theory: An Indigenous Feminist Approach to Affect and History." *Wicazo Ša Review* 24, no. 2 (Fall 2009): 53–76.

———. *Therapeutic Nations: Healing in an Age of Indigenous Human Rights.* Tucson: University of Arizona Press, 2013.

———. "There Is a River in Me: Theory from Life." In *Theorizing Native Studies,* edited by Audra Simpson and Andrea Smith, 31–42. Durham, NC: Duke University Press, 2014.

Mitchell, Terry, Courtney Arseneau, and Darren Thomas. "Colonial Trauma: Complex, Continuous, Collective, Cumulative and Compounding Effects on the Health of Indigenous Peoples in Canada and Beyond." *International Journal of Indigenous Health* 14, no. 2 (2019): 74–94. https://jps.library.utoronto.ca/index.php/ijih /article/view/32251/25279.

Mohatta, Nathaniel Vincent, Azure B. Thompson, Nghi D. Thaib, and Jacob Kraemer Tebesa. "Historical Trauma as Public Narrative: A Conceptual Review of How History Impacts Present-Day Health." *Social Science and Medicine* (April 2014): 128–36.

Morrison, Dawn. "Indigenous Food Sovereignty: A Model for Social Learning." In *Food Sovereignty in Canada: Creating Just and Sustainable Food Systems*, edited by Hannah Wittman, Annette Aurélie Desmarais, and Nettie Wiebe, 97–113. Winnipeg: Fernwood Publishing, 2011.

———. Personal communication, December 21, 2019.

———. Planning for Indigenous Social and Ecological Resilience in Times of COVID-19 and Climate Crisis. May 5, 2020. http://www.indigenousfoodsystems.org /content/planning-indigenous-social-and-ecological-resilience-times-covid-19-and -climate-crisis.

Morrow, Shayne. "Canada Must Apologize for Nutritional Experiments at Residential School: Tseshaht." *Ha-Shilth-Sa*, July 17, 2013. http://www.hashilthsa.com /news/2013-07-17/canada-must-apologize-nutritional-experiments-residential -school-tseshaht.

———. "40th Year Shaping Up." *Ha-Shilth-Sa*, July 27, 2016. https://hashilthsa.com /news/2016-07-27/40th-anniversary-celebration-shaping.

Mosby, Ian. "Administering Colonial Science: Nutrition Research and Human Biomedical Experimentation in Aboriginal Communities and Residential Schools, 1942–1952." *Social History* 46, no. 91 (May 2013): 145–72.

Mosby, Ian, and Tracey Galloway. "'Hunger Was Never Absent': How Residential School Diets Shaped Current Patterns of Diabetes among Indigenous Peoples in Canada." *Medicine and Society, Humanities* 189, no. 32 (August 14, 2017): 1043–45.

Moss, Michael. *Salt, Sugar, Fat: How the Food Giants Hooked Us*. New York: Random House, 2013.

The Muckleshoot Food Sovereignty Program. http://communityfood.wkkf.org /stories-of-innovation/muckleshoot-food-sovereignty/. Accessed June 20, 2019.

Native American Food Sovereignty Alliance (NAFSA) website. https://nativefood alliance.org/. Accessed April 2020.

Navajo Department of Health. "Dikos Ntsaaígíí-19 (COVID-19)." https://www.ndoh .navajo-nsn.gov/covid-19. Accessed January 21, 2021.

The Northwest Indian College Traditional Plants and Foods Program. https://www .nwic.edu/community/traditional-plants-and-foods/. Accessed June 20, 2019.

The Nuu-chah-nulth Research and Litigation Project, NTC website. http://www .nuuchahnulth.org/tribalcouncil/fisheries.html.

An Overview of Aboriginal Health in Canada. National Collaborating Centre for Aboriginal Health, Statistics Canada, Prince George: University of Northern British Columbia, 2013. https://www.ccnsa-nccah.ca/docs/context/FS-Overview AbororiginalHealth-EN.pdf.

Patel, Raj. "Food Sovereignty." *Journal of Peasant Studies* 36 (2009): 663–706.

Plummer, Eric. "Tseshaht Community Garden Adds 30 Fruit Trees to Growing Collection." *Ha-Shilth-Sa*, September 24, 2018. https://hashilthsa.com/news /2018-09-24/tseshaht-community-garden-adds-30-fruit-trees-growing-collection.

Pollan, Michael. *In Defense of Food: An Eater's Manifesto.* New York: Penguin Books, 2008.

——. *The Omnivore's Dilemma: A Natural History of Four Meals.* New York: Penguin Books, 2006.

Powell, Jay, ed. *Our World, Our Ways: Ṫaaṫaaqsapa Cultural Dictionary.* Port Alberni, BC: Nuu-chah-nulth Tribal Council, 1991.

Preston, čiisma Della. Personal communication, January 17, 2021.

Puxley, Chinta. "Up to 6,000 Children Died at Canada's Residential Schools, Report Finds." Global News website, May 31, 2015. https://globalnews.ca/news/2027587 /deaths-at-canadas-indian-residential-schools-need-more-study-commission/.

Quinn, Susie. "Nuu-chah-nulth Nations on Vancouver Island Hit Hard by COVID-19." *Vancouver Island Free Daily,* December 1, 2020. https://www.vancouverisland freedaily.com/news/nuu-chah-nulth-nations-on-vancouver-island-hit-hard-by -covid-19/.

Rampanen, ṅaasʔałuk John. Personal communication, August 12, 2015; December 23, 2019.

Rampanen, Kalilah. Personal communication, December 23, 2019.

Raymond, Christopher M., Gerald G. Singh, Karina Benessaiah, Joanna R. Bernhardt, Jordan Levine, Harry Nelson, Nancy J. Turner, Bryan Norton, Jordan Tam, and Kai M. A. Chan. "Ecosystem Services and Beyond: Using Multiple Metaphors to Understand Human-Environment Relationships." *BioScience* 63, no. 7 (July 2013): 536–45.

Reyner, Jon, and Jeanne Eder. *American Indian Education: A History.* Norman: University of Oklahoma Press, 2004.

Robinson, Anne. Personal communication, August 11, 2015.

Rosman, Abraham, and Paula G. Rubel. *Feasting with Mine Enemy: Rank and Exchange among Northwest Coast Society.* Long Grove, IL: Waveland Press, 1971.

Ross, Darrell, Sr. Personal communication, August 11, 2015.

Rosset, Peter. "Food Sovereignty and the Contemporary Food Crisis." *Development* 51 (2008): 460–63.

Salmón, Enrique. *Eating the Landscape: American Indians Stories of Food, Identity, and Resilience.* Tucson: University of Arizona Press, 2012.

Sam, Les. Personal communication, August 11, 2015.

Sam, Richard, Jr. Personal communication, August 11, 2015.

Sapir, Edward, and Morris Swadesh. *Native Accounts of Nootka Ethnography.* Publication no. 1. Bloomington: Indiana University Research Center in Anthropology, Folklore, and Linguistics, 1955.

——. *Nootka Texts: Tales and Ethnological Narratives.* Philadelphia: University of Pennsylvania, 1939.

Sheehy, Tony, Cindy Roache, and Sangita Sharma. "Eating Habits of a Population Undergoing a Rapid Dietary Transition: Portion Sizes of Traditional and Non-traditional Foods and Beverages Consumed by Inuit Adults in Nunavut, Canada." *Nutrition Journal* 12, no. 17 (2013): 1–11.

Shiva, Vandana. "Food Sovereignty, Food Security." In *Seed Sovereignty: Food Security. Women in the Vanguard of the Fight against GMOs and Corporate Agriculture*, vii–xii. Berkeley, CA: North Atlantic Books, 2016.

Shukla, Shailesh, and Priscilla Settee, eds. *Indigenous Food Systems: Concepts, Cases, and Conversations*. Toronto: Canadian Scholars, 2020.

Sium, Aman, Chandni Desai, and Eric Ritskes. "Towards the 'Tangible Unknown': Decolonization and the Indigenous Future." *Decolonization: Indigeneity, Education and Society* 1, no. 12 (2012): i–xiii, open access. https://jps.library.utoronto.ca /index.php/des/article/view/18638/15564.

Sium, Aman, and Eric Ritskes. "Speaking Truth to Power: Indigenous Storytelling as an Act of Living Resistance." *Decolonization: Indigeneity, Education & Society* 2, no. 1 (2013): i–x.

Slow Food Turtle Island Association Facebook page. https://www.facebook.com/Slow foodturtleisland/. Accessed May 5, 2020.

Smith, Andrea. *Indigenous Peoples and Boarding Schools: A Comparative Study*. Prepared for the Secretariat of the United Nations Permanent Forum on Indigenous Issues, January 2009. https://www.un.org/esa/socdev/unpfii/documents/E_C_19_2009 _crp1.pdf.

Smith, Linda Tuhiwai. *Decolonizing Methodologies: Research and Indigenous Peoples*. 2nd ed. London: Zed Books, 2012.

Sproat, Gilbert M. *Scenes and Studies of Savage Life*. London: Smith, Elder and Company, 1868.

Statement by the NGO Forum to the World Food Summit. *World Food Summit*, November 13–17, 1996. http://www.fao.org/wfs/. Accessed September 25, 2015.

St. Claire, Denis E. "Barkley Sound Tribal Territories." In E. Y. Arima, Denis St. Claire, Louis Clamhouse, Joshua Edgar, Charles Jones, and John Thomas, *Between Ports Alberni and Renfrew: Notes on West Coast Peoples*. Hull, QC: Canadian Museum of Civilization, 1991.

Stewart, Hilary. *Cedar*. Seattle: University of Washington Press, 1984.

———. *Indian Fishing: Early Methods on the Northwest Coast*. Vancouver: Douglas & McIntire, 1977.

Story, Mary, Marguerite Evans, Richard R. Fabsitz, Theresa E. Clay, Bonnie Holy Rock, and Brenda Broussard. "The Epidemic of Obesity in American Indian Communities and the Need for Childhood Obesity-Prevention Programs." *American Journal of Clinical Nutrition* 69 (1999): 747–54.

Strong Heart Study, 2001 Report. National Institutes of Health, 2001. https://www.nhlbi .nih.gov/files/docs/public/heart/shs_db.pdf.

Thomas, Linda. Personal communication, August 11, 2015.

Thomas, Megan. "17 Fish Farms Could All Be Phased Out under New Agreement between B.C. Government, First Nations." *CBC News*, December 14, 2018. https://www.cbc.ca/news/canada/british-columbia/bc-fish-farms-broughton -archipelago-1.4946570.

Thomas, Shaunee. Personal communication, January 6, 2020.

Titian, Denise. "Family Makes 'Indian Medicine' to Help Isolated Community through Pandemic Restrictions." *Ha-Shilth-Sa*, December 8, 2020. https://hashilthsa.com/news/2020-12-08/family-makes-indian-medicine-help -isolated-community-through-pandemic-restrictions.

———. "Reclaiming Lost Souls of the Alberni Indian Residential School." *Ha-Shilth-Sa*, September 27, 2019. https://hashilthsa.com/news/2019-09-27 /reclaiming-lost-souls-alberni-indian-residential-school-healing-event-draws -hundreds.

Traditional Nuu-chah-nulth Food Harvesting and Preparation, Native Studies Program, School District No. 70 (Alberni).

Trauger, Amy. "Putting Food Sovereignty in Place." In *Food Sovereignty in International Context: Discourse, Politics and Practice of Place*, edited by Amy Trauger, 1–12. New York: Routledge, 2015.

Truth and Reconciliation Commission (TRC). *Honouring the Truth, Reconciling for the Future: Summary of the Final Report of the Truth and Reconciliation Commission of Canada.* 2015 Report. TRC website. http://www.trc.ca/.

Tuck, Eve, and K. Wayne Yang. "Decolonization Is Not a Metaphor." *Decolonization, Indigeneity, Education & Society* 1, no. 1 (2012): 1–40.

Turner, Nancy J. *The Earth's Blanket: Traditional Teachings for Sustainable Living.* Seattle: University of Washington Press, 2005.

Turner, Nancy, Marianne Boelscher Ignace, and Ronald Ignace. "Traditional Ecological Knowledge and Wisdom of Aboriginal Peoples in British Columbia." *Ecological Applications* 10, no. 5 (October 2000): 1275–87.

Turner, Nancy J., Mark Plotkin, and Harriet V. Kuhnlein. "Global Environmental Challenges to the Integrity of Indigenous Peoples' Food Systems." In *Indigenous Peoples' Food Systems & Well-Being: Interventions & Policies for Healthy Communities*, edited by V. Harriet Kuhnlein, Bill Erasmus, Dina Spigelski, and Barbara Burlingame, 23–38. Rome: Food and Agriculture Organization of the United Nations & Centre for Indigenous Peoples' Nutrition and Environment, 2013.

Turner, Nancy J., and Katherine L. Turner. "'Where Our Women Used to Get the Food': Cumulative Effects and Loss of Ethnobotanical Knowledge and Practice; Case Study from Coastal British Columbia." *Botany* 86 (2008): 103–15.

Two Horses, Michael. "'We Know Who the Real Indians Are': Animal-Rights Groups, Racial Stereotyping, and Racism in Rhetoric and Action in the Makah Whaling Controversy." Master's thesis, University of Arizona, 2001.

United Nations Declaration on the Rights of Indigenous Peoples, 2007. http://www .un.org/esa/socdev/unpfii/documents/DRIPS_en.pdf.

United Nations Food and Agricultural Organization (FAO), Committee on World Food Security, Global Strategic Framework (GSF). http://www.fao.org/cfs/home /products/onlinegsf/1/en/. Accessed January 2, 2021.

Uu-a-thluk website. https://uuathluk.ca/about/. Accessed January 12, 2019.

Uu-a-thluk Strategic Plan: Building on Our Successes 2018–2023. http://uuathluk.ca /wordpress/wp-content/uploads/2018/03/Uu-a-thluk-Strategic-Plan-2018-2023 .pdf. Accessed January 12, 2019.

Vancouver Island & Coastal Communities Indigenous Foods Network (VICCIFN). https://indigenousfoods.docu.li/#:~:text=The%20Vancouver%20Island%20 %26%20Coastal%20Communities,Nations%20cultural%20teachings%20and%20 practices. Accessed March 15, 2020.

"Warrior Society Dissolves." *Globe and Mail,* August 4, 2005. https://www.theglobe andmail.com/news/national/warrior-society-dissolves/article18242623/.

Watts, Cathy. Personal communication, August 11, 2015.

Waziyatawin. "The Paradox of Indigenous Resurgence at the End of Empire." *Decolonization: Indigeneity, Education & Society* 1, no. 1 (2012): 68–85.

Weinberger, Hannah. "Still Recovering from Escaped Atlantic Salmon, Cooke Aquaculture Now Wants to Farm Steelhead." *Crosscut,* August 5, 2019. https://crosscut.com/2019/08/still-recovering-escaped-atlantic-salmon-cooke -aquaculture-now-wants-farm-steelhead.

Werle, ƛiisƛiisaʔapt Adam. Personal communication, August 17, September 7, October 24, November 11, 2020; January 4, 5, 17, 30, 2021.

White Earth Land Recovery Project website. https://www.welrp.org/. Accessed July 20, 2019.

Whyte, Kyle Powys. "Food Sovereignty, Justice and Indigenous Peoples: An Essay on Settler Colonialism and Collective Continuance." In *Oxford Handbook of Food Ethics,* edited by A. Barnhill, T. Doggett, and A. Egan, 1–21. Oxford, UK: Oxford University Press, 2017.

Wild Salmon Caravan website. https://wildsalmoncaravan.ca/. Accessed July 11, 2020.

Wittman, Hannah, Annette Aurélie Desmarais, and Nettie Wiebe. "The Origins and Potential of Food Sovereignty." In *Food Sovereignty: Reconnecting Food, Nature and Community,* edited by Hannah Wittman, Annette Aurélie Desmarais, and Nettie Wiebe, 1–14. Winnipeg: Fernwood Publishing, 2010.

Women's Earth Alliance and Native Youth Sexual Health Network. *Violence on Our Lands, Violence on Our Bodies: Building an Indigenous Response to Environmental Violence.* Berkeley, CA: David Brower Center, 2016.

INDEX

fig. after a page reference denotes an illustration.
map after a page reference denotes a map.

ABOUT THE AUTHOR

Dr. Charlotte Coté is from the Nuu-chah-nulth community of Tseshaht on the west coast of Vancouver Island. She is associate professor in American Indian Studies at the University of Washington and serves as co-editor for the University of Washington Press's Indigenous Confluences Series.

Dr. Coté has dedicated her personal and academic life to creating awareness around Indigenous health and wellness issues and working with Indigenous peoples and communities in revitalizing their traditional foodways. She is the author of *Spirits of Our Whaling Ancestors: Revitalizing Makah and Nuu-chah-nulth Traditions* (UW Press, 2010). Dr. Coté is the founder and chair of the UW's annual The Living Breath of wǝɫǝbʔaltxʷ Indigenous Foods Symposium.

 Indigenous Confluences

Charlotte Coté and Coll Thrush, *Series Editors*

Indigenous Confluences publishes innovative works that use decolonizing perspectives and transnational approaches to explore the experiences of Indigenous peoples across North America, with special emphasis on the Pacific Coast.

A Chemehuevi Song: The Resilience of a Southern Paiute Tribe
by Clifford E. Trafzer

Education at the Edge of Empire: Negotiating Pueblo Identity in New Mexico's Indian Boarding Schools
by John R. Gram

Indian Blood: HIV and Colonial Trauma in San Francisco's Two-Spirit Community
by Andrew J. Jolivette

Native Students at Work: American Indian Labor and Sherman Institute's Outing Program, 1900–1945
by Kevin Whalen

California through Native Eyes: Reclaiming History
by William J. Bauer Jr.

Unlikely Alliances: Native Nations and White Communities Join to Defend Rural Lands
by Zoltán Grossman

Dismembered: Native Disenrollment and the Battle for Human Rights
by David E. Wilkins and Shelly Hulse Wilkins

Network Sovereignty: Building the Internet across Indian Country
by Marisa Elena Duarte

Chinook Resilience: Heritage and Cultural Revitalization on the Lower Columbia River
by Jon Daehnke

Power in the Telling: Grand Ronde, Warm Springs, and Intertribal Relations in the Casino Era
by Brook Colley

We Are Dancing for You: Native Feminisms and the Revitalization of Women's Coming-of-Age Ceremonies
by Cutcha Risling Baldy

A Drum in One Hand, a Sockeye in the Other: Stories of Indigenous Food Sovereignty from the Northwest Coast
by Charlotte Coté